FDR

Selected Speeches of
President Franklin D Roosevelt

Red and Black Publishers, St Petersburg, Florida

Library of Congress Cataloging-in-Publication Data

Roosevelt, Franklin D. (Franklin Delano), 1882-1945
   FDR : selected speeches of president Franklin D Roosevelt / by Franklin D
Roosevelt.
        p. cm.
   ISBN 978-1-934941-97-3
1. United States--Politics and government--1933-1945--Sources. 2. United States--
Foreign relations--1933-1945--Sources. 3. Roosevelt, Franklin D. (Franklin Delano),
1882-1945--Oratory. 4. Speeches, addresses, etc., American. I. Title.
   J82.D6 2010
   352.23'80973--dc22

                                                        2010022806

Red and Black Publishers, PO Box 7542, St Petersburg, Florida, 33734

Contact us at: info@RedandBlackPublishers.com

         Printed and manufactured in the United States of America

Contents

Acceptance Speech at the 1932 Democratic National Convention

"The greatest good to the greatest number of our citizens".

(July 2, 1932)

Chairman Walsh, my friends of the Democratic National Convention of 1932:

I appreciate your willingness after these six arduous days to remain here, for I know well the sleepless hours which you and I have had. I regret that I am late, but I have no control over the winds of Heaven and could only be thankful for my Navy training.

The appearance before a National Convention of its nominee for President, to be formally notified of his selection, is unprecedented and unusual, but these are unprecedented and unusual times. I have started out on the tasks that lie ahead by breaking the absurd traditions that the candidate should remain in professed ignorance of what has happened for weeks until he is formally notified of that event many weeks later.

My friends, may this be the symbol of my intention to be honest and to avoid all hypocrisy or sham, to avoid all silly shutting of the eyes to the truth in this campaign. You have nominated me and I know it, and I am here to thank you for the honor.

Let it also be symbolic that in so doing I broke traditions. Let it be from now on the task of our Party to break foolish traditions. We will break foolish traditions and leave it to the Republican leadership, far more skilled in that art, to break promises.

Let us now and here highly resolve to resume the country's interrupted march along the path of real progress, of real justice, of real equality for all of our citizens, great and small. Our indomitable leader in that interrupted march is no longer with us, but there still survives today his spirit. Many of his captains, thank God, are still with us, to give us wise counsel. Let us feel that in everything we do there still lives with us, if not the body, the great indomitable, unquenchable, progressive soul of our Commander-in-Chief, Woodrow Wilson.

I have many things on which I want to make my position clear at the earliest possible moment in this campaign. That admirable document, the platform which you have adopted, is clear. I accept it 100 percent.

And you can accept my pledge that I will leave no doubt or ambiguity on where I stand on any question of moment in this campaign.

As we enter this new battle, let us keep always present with us some of the ideals of the Party: The fact that the Democratic Party by tradition and by the continuing logic of history, past and present, is the bearer of liberalism and of progress and at the same time of safety to our institutions. And if this appeal fails, remember well, my friends, that a resentment against the failure of Republican leadership—and note well that in this campaign I shall not use the word "Republican Party," but I shall use, day in and day out, the words, "Republican leadership" — the failure of Republican leaders to solve our troubles may degenerate into unreasoning radicalism.

The great social phenomenon of this depression, unlike others before it, is that it has produced but a few of the disorderly manifestations that too often attend upon such times.

Wild radicalism has made few converts, and the greatest tribute that I can pay to my countrymen is that in these days of crushing want there persists an orderly and hopeful spirit on the part of the millions of our people who have suffered so much. To fail to offer them a new chance is not only to betray their hopes but to misunderstand their patience.

To meet by reaction that danger of radicalism is to invite disaster. Reaction is no barrier to the radical. It is a challenge, a provocation. The way to meet that danger is to offer a workable program of reconstruction, and the party to offer it is the party with clean hands.

This, and this only, is a proper protection against blind reaction on the one hand and an improvised, hit-or-miss, irresponsible opportunism on the other.

There are two ways of viewing the Government's duty in matters affecting economic and social life. The first sees to it that a favored few are helped and hopes that some of their prosperity will leak through, sift through, to labor, to the farmer, to the small business man. That theory belongs to the party of Toryism, and I had hoped that most of the Tories left this country in 1776

But it is not and never will be the theory of the Democratic Party. This is no time for fear, for reaction or for timidity. Here and now I invite those nominal Republicans who find that their conscience cannot be squared with the groping and the failure of their party leaders to join hands with us; here and now, in equal measure, I warn those nominal Democrats who squint at the future with their faces turned toward the past, and who feel no responsibility to the demands of the new time, that they are out of step with their Party.

Yes, the people of this country want a genuine choice this year, not a choice between two names for the same reactionary doctrine. Ours must be a party of liberal thought, of planned action, of enlightened international outlook, and of the greatest good to the greatest number of our citizens.

Now it is inevitable—and the choice is that of the times—it is inevitable that the main issue of this campaign should revolve about the clear fact of our economic condition, a depression so deep that it is without precedent in modern history. It will not do merely to state, as do Republican leaders to explain their broken promises of continued inaction, that the depression is worldwide. That was not their explanation of the apparent prosperity of 1928. The people will not forget the claim made by them then that prosperity was only a domestic product manufactured by a Republican President and a Republican Congress. If they claim paternity for the one they cannot deny paternity for the other.

I cannot take up all the problems today. I want to touch on a few that are vital. Let us look a little at the recent history and the simple economics, the kind of economics that you and I and the average man and woman talk.

In the years before 1929 we know that this country had completed a vast cycle of building and inflation; for ten years we expanded on the theory of repairing the wastes of the War, but actually expanding far beyond that, and also beyond our natural and normal growth. Now it is worth remembering, and the cold figures of finance prove it, that during that time there was little or no drop in the prices that the consumer had to pay, although those same figures proved that the cost of production fell very greatly; corporate profit resulting from this period was enormous; at the same time little of that profit was devoted to the reduction of prices. The consumer was forgotten. Very little of it went into increased wages; the worker was forgotten, and by no means an adequate proportion was even paid out in dividends—the stockholder was forgotten.

And, incidentally, very little of it was taken by taxation to the beneficent Government of those years.

What was the result? Enormous corporate surpluses piled up—the most stupendous in history. Where, under the spell of delirious speculation, did those surpluses go? Let us talk economics that the figures prove and that we can understand. Why, they went chiefly in two directions: first, into new and unnecessary plants which now stand stark and idle; and second, into the call-money market of Wall Street, either directly by the corporations, or indirectly through the banks. Those are the facts. Why blink at them?

Then came the crash. You know the story. Surpluses invested in unnecessary plants became idle. Men lost their jobs; purchasing power dried up; banks became frightened and started calling loans. Those who had money were afraid to part with it. Credit contracted. Industry stopped. Commerce declined, and unemployment mounted.

And there we are today.

Translate that into human terms. See how the events of the past three years have come home to specific groups of people: first, the group dependent on industry; second, the group dependent on agriculture; third, and made up in large part of members of the first two groups, the people who are called "small investors and depositors." In fact, the strongest possible tie between the first two groups, agriculture and industry, is the fact that the savings and to a degree the security of both are tied together in that third group—the credit structure of the Nation.

Never in history have the interests of all the people been so united in a single economic problem. Picture to yourself, for instance, the great groups of property owned by millions of our citizens, represented by credits issued in the form of bonds and mortgages—Government bonds of all kinds, Federal, State, county, municipal; bonds of industrial companies, of utility companies; mortgages on real estate in farms and cities, and finally the vast investments of the Nation in the railroads. What is the measure of the security of each of those groups? We know well that in our complicated, interrelated credit structure if any one of these credit groups collapses they may all collapse. Danger to one is danger to all.

How, I ask, has the present Administration in Washington treated the interrelationship of these credit groups? The answer is clear: It has not recognized that interrelationship existed at all. Why, the Nation asks, has Washington failed to understand that all of these groups, each and every one, the top of the pyramid and the bottom of the pyramid, must be considered together, that each and every one of them is dependent on every other; each and every one of them affecting the whole financial fabric?

Statesmanship and vision, my friends, require relief to all at the same time.

Just one word or two on taxes, the taxes that all of us pay toward the cost of Government of all kinds.

I know something of taxes. For three long years I have been going up and down this country preaching that Government — Federal and State and local — costs too much. I shall not stop that preaching. As an immediate program of action we must abolish useless offices. We must eliminate unnecessary functions of Government — functions, in fact, that are not definitely essential to the continuance of Government. We must merge, we must consolidate subdivisions of Government, and, like the private citizen, give up luxuries which we can no longer afford.

By our example at Washington itself, we shall have the opportunity of pointing the way of economy to local government, for let us remember well that out of every tax dollar in the average State in this Nation, 40 cents enter the treasury in Washington, D. C., 10 or 12 cents only go to the State capitals, and 48 cents are consumed by the costs of local government in counties and cities and towns.

I propose to you, my friends, and through you, that Government of all kinds, big and little, be made solvent and that the example be set by the President of the United States and his Cabinet.

And talking about setting a definite example, I congratulate this convention for having had the courage fearlessly to write into its declaration of principles what an overwhelming majority here assembled really thinks about the 18th Amendment. This convention wants repeal. Your candidate wants repeal. And I am confident that the United States of America wants repeal.

Two years ago the platform on which I ran for Governor the second time contained substantially the same provision. The overwhelming sentiment of the people of my State, as shown by the vote of that year, extends, I know, to the people of many of the other States. I say to you now that from this date on the 18th Amendment is doomed. When that happens, we as Democrats must and will, rightly and morally, enable the States to protect themselves against the importation of intoxicating liquor where such importation may violate their State laws. We must rightly and morally prevent the return of the saloon.

To go back to this dry subject of finance, because it all ties in together — the 18th Amendment has something to do with finance, too — in a comprehensive planning for the reconstruction of the great credit groups, including Government credit, I list an important place for that prize statement of principle in the platform here adopted calling for the letting in of the light of day on issues of securities, foreign and domestic, which are offered for sale to the investing public.

My friends, you and I as common-sense citizens know that it would help to protect the savings of the country from the dishonesty of crooks and from the lack of honor of some men in high financial places. Publicity is the enemy of crookedness.

And now one word about unemployment, and incidentally about agriculture. I have favored the use of certain types of public works as a further emergency means of stimulating employment and the issuance of bonds to pay for such public works, but I have pointed out that no economic end is served if we merely build without building for a necessary purpose. Such works, of course, should insofar as possible be self-sustaining if they are to be financed by the issuing of bonds. So as to spread the points of all kinds as widely as possible, we must take definite steps to shorten the working day and the working week.

Let us use common sense and business sense. Just as one example, we know that a very hopeful and immediate means of relief, both for the unemployed and for agriculture, will come from a wide plan of the converting of many millions of acres of marginal and unused land into timberland through reforestation. There are tens of millions of acres east of the Mississippi River alone in abandoned farms, in cut-over land, now growing up in worthless brush. Why, every European Nation has a definite land policy, and has had one for generations. We have none. Having none, we face a future of soil erosion and timber famine. It is clear that economic foresight and immediate employment march hand in hand in the call for the reforestation of these vast areas.

In so doing, employment can be given to a million men. That is the kind of public work that is self-sustaining, and therefore capable of being financed by the issuance of bonds which are made secure by the fact that the growth of tremendous crops will provide adequate security for the investment.

Yes, I have a very definite program for providing employment by that means. I have done it, and I am doing it today in the State of New York. I know that the Democratic Party can do it successfully in the Nation. That will put men to work, and that is an example of the action that we are going to have.

Now as a further aid to agriculture, we know perfectly well — but have we come out and said so clearly and distinctly? — we should repeal immediately those provisions of law that compel the Federal Government to go into the market to purchase, to sell, to speculate in farm products in a futile attempt to reduce farm surpluses. And they are the people who are talking of keeping Government out of business. The practical way to help the farmer is by an arrangement that will, in addition to lightening some of the impoverishing burdens from his back, do something toward the reduction of the surpluses of staple commodities that hang on the market. It should be our aim to add to the world prices of staple products the amount of a reasonable tariff protection, to give agriculture the same protection that industry has today.

And in exchange for this immediately increased return I am sure that the farmers of this Nation would agree ultimately to such planning of their production as would reduce the surpluses and make it unnecessary in later years to depend on dumping those surpluses abroad in order to support domestic prices. That result has been accomplished in other Nations; why not in America, too?

Farm leaders and farm economists, generally, agree that a plan based on that principle is a desirable first step in the reconstruction of agriculture. It does not in itself furnish a complete program, but it will serve in great measure in the long run to remove the pall of a surplus without the continued perpetual threat of world dumping. Final voluntary reduction of surplus is a part of our objective, but the long continuance and the present burden of existing surpluses make it necessary to repair great damage of the present by immediate emergency measures.

Such a plan as that, my friends, does not cost the Government any money, nor does it keep the Government in business or in speculation.

As to the actual wording of a bill, I believe that the Democratic Party stands ready to be guided by whatever the responsible farm groups themselves agree on. That is a principle that is sound; and again I ask for action.

One more word about the farmer, and I know that every delegate in this hall who lives in the city knows why I lay emphasis on the farmer. It is because one-half of our population, over 50,000,000 people, are dependent on agriculture; and, my friends, if those 50,000,000 people have no money, no cash, to buy what is produced in the city, the city suffers to an equal or greater extent.

That is why we are going to make the voters understand this year that this Nation is not merely a Nation of independence, but it is, if we are to survive, bound to be a Nation of interdependence—town and city, and North and South, East and West. That is our goal, and that goal will be understood by the people of this country no matter where they live.

Yes, the purchasing power of that half of our population dependent on agriculture is gone. Farm mortgages reach nearly ten billions of dollars today and interest charges on that alone are $560,000,000 a year. But that is not all. The tax burden caused by extravagant and inefficient local government is an additional factor. Our most immediate concern should be to reduce the interest burden on these mortgages.

Rediscounting of farm mortgages under salutary restrictions must be expanded and should, in the future, be conditioned on the reduction of interest rates. Amortization payments, maturities should likewise in this crisis be extended before rediscount is permitted where the mortgagor is sorely pressed. That, my friends, is another example of practical, immediate relief: Action.

I aim to do the same thing, and it can be done, for the small home-owner in our cities and villages. We can lighten his burden and develop his purchasing power. Take away, my friends, that spectre of too high an interest rate. Take away that spectre of the due date just a short time away. Save homes; save homes for thousands of self-respecting families, and drive out that spectre of insecurity from our midst.

Out of all the tons of printed paper, out of all the hours of oratory, the recriminations, the defenses, the happy-thought plans in Washington and in every State, there emerges one great, simple, crystal-pure fact that during the past ten years a Nation of 120,000,000 people has been led by the Republican leaders to erect an impregnable barbed wire entanglement around its borders through the instrumentality of tariffs which have isolated us from all the other human beings in all the rest of the round world. I accept that admirable tariff statement in the platform of this convention. It would protect American business and American labor. By our acts of the past we have invited and received the retaliation of other Nations. I propose an invitation to them to forget the past, to sit at the table with us, as friends, and to plan with us for the restoration of the trade of the world.

Go into the home of the business man. He knows what the tariff has done for him. Go into the home of the factory worker. He knows why goods do not move. Go into the home of the farmer. He knows how the tariff has helped to ruin him.

At last our eyes are open. At last the American people are ready to acknowledge that Republican leadership was wrong and that the Democracy is right.

My program, of which I can only touch on these points, is based upon this simple moral principle: the welfare and the soundness of a Nation depend first upon what the great mass of the people wish and need; and second, whether or not they are getting it.

What do the people of America want more than anything else? To my mind, they want two things: work, with all the moral and spiritual values that go with it; and with work, a reasonable measure of security — security for themselves and for their wives and children. Work and security — these are more than words. They are more than facts. They are the spiritual values, the true goal toward which our efforts of reconstruction should lead. These are the values that this program is intended to gain; these are the values we have failed to achieve by the leadership we now have.

Our Republican leaders tell us economic laws — sacred, inviolable, unchangeable — cause panics which no one could prevent. But while they prate of economic laws, men and women are starving. We must lay hold of the fact that economic laws are not made by nature. They are made by human beings.

Yes, when — not if — when we get the chance, the Federal Government will assume bold leadership in distress relief. For years Washington has alternated between putting its head in the sand and saying there is no large number of destitute people in our midst who need food and clothing, and then saying the States should take care of them, if there are. Instead of planning two and a half years ago to do what they are now trying to do, they kept putting it off from day to day, week to week, and month to month, until the conscience of America demanded action.

I say that while primary responsibility for relief rests with localities now, as ever, yet the Federal Government has always had and still has a continuing responsibility for the broader public welfare. It will soon fulfill that responsibility.

And now, just a few words about our plans for the next four months. By coming here instead of waiting for a formal notification, I have made it clear that I believe we should eliminate expensive ceremonies and that we should set in motion at once, tonight, my friends, the necessary machinery for an adequate presentation of the issues to the electorate of the Nation.

I myself have important duties as Governor of a great State, duties which in these times are more arduous and more grave than at any previous period. Yet I feel confident that I shall be able to make a number of short visits to several parts of the Nation. My trips will have as their first objective the study at first hand, from the lips of men and women of all parties and all occupations, of the actual conditions and needs of every part of an interdependent country.

One word more: Out of every crisis, every tribulation, every disaster, mankind rises with some share of greater knowledge, of higher decency, of purer purpose. Today we shall have come through a period of loose thinking, descending morals, an era of selfishness, among individual men and women and among Nations. Blame not Governments alone for this. Blame ourselves in equal share. Let us be frank in acknowledgment of the truth that many amongst us have made obeisance to Mammon, that the profits of speculation, the easy road without toil, have lured us from the old barricades. To return to higher standards we must abandon the false prophets and seek new leaders of our own choosing.

Never before in modern history have the essential differences between the two major American parties stood out in such striking contrast as they do today. Republican leaders not only have failed in material things, they have failed in national vision, because in disaster they have held out no hope, they have pointed out no path for the people below to climb back to places of security and of safety in our American life.

Throughout the Nation, men and women, forgotten in the political philosophy of the Government of the last years look to us here for guidance and for more equitable opportunity to share in the distribution of national wealth.

On the farms, in the large metropolitan areas, in the smaller cities and in the villages, millions of our citizens cherish the hope that their old standards of living and of thought have not gone forever. Those millions cannot and shall not hope in vain.

I pledge you, I pledge myself, to a new deal for the American people. Let us all here assembled constitute ourselves prophets of a new order of competence and of courage. This is more than a political campaign; it is a call to arms. Give me your help, not to win votes alone, but to win in this crusade to restore America to its own people.

First Inaugural Address

"The only thing we have to fear is — fear itself."

(March 4, 1933)

President Hoover, Mr. Chief Justice, my friends:

This is a day of national consecration. And I am certain that on this day my fellow Americans expect that on my induction into the Presidency I will address them with a candor and a decision which the present situation of our people impels. This is preeminently the time to speak the truth, the whole truth, frankly and boldly. Nor need we shrink from honestly facing conditions in our country today. This great Nation will endure as it has endured, will revive and will prosper. So, first of all, let me assert my firm belief that the only thing we have to fear is fear itself — nameless, unreasoning, unjustified terror which paralyzes needed efforts to convert retreat into advance. In every dark hour of our national life a leadership of frankness and vigor has met with that understanding and support of the people themselves which is essential to victory. I am convinced that you will again give that support to leadership in these critical days.

In such a spirit on my part and on yours we face our common difficulties. They concern, thank God, only material things. Values have shrunken to fantastic levels; taxes have risen; our ability to pay has fallen; government of all kinds is faced by serious curtailment of income; the means of exchange are frozen in the currents of trade; the withered leaves of industrial enterprise lie on every side; farmers find no markets for their produce; the savings of many years in thousands of families are gone.

More important, a host of unemployed citizens face the grim problem of existence, and an equally great number toil with little return. Only a foolish optimist can deny the dark realities of the moment.

Yet our distress comes from no failure of substance. We are stricken by no plague of locusts. Compared with the perils which our forefathers conquered because they believed and were not afraid, we have still much to be thankful for. Nature still offers her bounty and human efforts have multiplied it. Plenty is at our doorstep, but a generous use of it languishes in the very sight of the supply. Primarily this is because rulers of the exchange of mankind's goods have failed through their own stubbornness and their own incompetence, have admitted their failure, and have abdicated. Practices of the unscrupulous money-changers stand indicted in the court of public opinion, rejected by the hearts and minds of men.

True they have tried, but their efforts have been cast in the pattern of an outworn tradition. Faced by failure of credit they have proposed only the lending of more money. Stripped of the lure of profit by which to induce our people to follow their false leadership, they have resorted to exhortations, pleading tearfully for restored confidence. They know only the rules of a generation of self-seekers. They have no vision, and when there is no vision the people perish.

The money-changers have fled from their high seats in the temple of our civilization. We may now restore that temple to the ancient truths. The measure of the restoration lies in the extent to which we apply social values more noble than mere monetary profit.

Happiness lies not in the mere possession of money; it lies in the joy of achievement, in the thrill of creative effort. The joy and moral stimulation of work no longer must be forgotten in the mad chase of evanescent profits. These dark days will be worth all they cost us if they teach us that our true destiny is not to be ministered unto but to minister to ourselves and to our fellow men.

Recognition of the falsity of material wealth as the standard of success goes hand in hand with the abandonment of the false belief that public office and high political position are to be valued only by the standards of pride of place and personal profit; and there must be an end to a conduct in banking and in business which too often has given to a sacred trust the likeness of callous and selfish wrongdoing. Small wonder that confidence languishes, for it thrives only on honesty, on honor, on the sacredness of obligations, on faithful protection, on unselfish performance; without them it cannot live. Restoration calls, however, not for changes in ethics alone. This Nation asks for action, and action now.

Our greatest primary task is to put people to work. This is no unsolvable problem if we face it wisely and courageously. It can be accomplished in part by direct recruiting by the Government itself, treating the task as we would treat the emergency of a war, but at the same time, through this employment, accomplishing greatly needed projects to stimulate and reorganize the use of our natural resources.

Hand in hand with this we must frankly recognize the overbalance of population in our industrial centers and, by engaging on a national scale in a redistribution, endeavor to provide a better use of the land for those best fitted for the land. The task can be helped by definite efforts to raise the values of agricultural products and with this the power to purchase the output of our cities. It can be helped by preventing realistically the tragedy of the growing loss through foreclosure of our small homes and our farms. It can be helped by insistence that the Federal, State, and local governments act forthwith on the demand that their cost be drastically reduced. It can be helped by the unifying of relief activities which today are often scattered, uneconomical, and unequal. It can be helped by national planning for and supervision of all forms of transportation and of communications and other utilities which have a definitely public character. There are many ways in which it can be helped, but it can never be helped merely by talking about it. We must act and act quickly.

Finally, in our progress toward a resumption of work we require two safeguards against a return of the evils of the old order: there must be a strict supervision of all banking and credits and investments, so that there will be an end to speculation with other people's money; and there must be provision for an adequate but sound currency.

These are the lines of attack. I shall presently urge upon a new Congress, in special session, detailed measures for their fulfillment, and I shall seek the immediate assistance of the several States.

Through this program of action we address ourselves to putting our own national house in order and making income balance outgo. Our international trade relations, though vastly important, are in point of time and necessity secondary to the establishment of a sound national economy. I favor as a practical policy the putting of first things first. I shall spare no effort to restore world trade by international economic readjustment, but the emergency at home cannot wait on that accomplishment.

The basic thought that guides these specific means of national recovery is not narrowly nationalistic. It is the insistence, as a first consideration, upon the interdependence of the various elements in and parts of the United States—a recognition of the old and permanently important manifestation of the American spirit of the pioneer. It is the way to recovery. It is the immediate way. It is the strongest assurance that the recovery will endure.

In the field of world policy I would dedicate this Nation to the policy of the good neighbor — the neighbor who resolutely respects himself and, because he does so, respects the rights of others — the neighbor who respects his obligations and respects the sanctity of his agreements in and with a world of neighbors.

If I read the temper of our people correctly, we now realize as we have never realized before our interdependence on each other; that we cannot merely take but we must give as well; that if we are to go forward, we must move as a trained and loyal army willing to sacrifice for the good of a common discipline, because without such discipline no progress is made, no leadership becomes effective. We are, I know, ready and willing to submit our lives and property to such discipline, because it makes possible a leadership which aims at a larger good. This I propose to offer, pledging that the larger purposes will bind upon us all as a sacred obligation with a unity of duty hitherto evoked only in time of armed strife.

With this pledge taken, I assume unhesitatingly the leadership of this great army of our people dedicated to a disciplined attack upon our common problems.

Action in this image and to this end is feasible under the form of government which we have inherited from our ancestors. Our Constitution is so simple and practical that it is possible always to meet extraordinary needs by changes in emphasis and arrangement without loss of essential form. That is why our constitutional system has proved itself the most superbly enduring political mechanism the modern world has produced. It has met every stress of vast expansion of territory, of foreign wars, of bitter internal strife, of world relations.

It is to be hoped that the normal balance of Executive and legislative authority may be wholly adequate to meet the unprecedented task before us. But it may be that an unprecedented demand and need for undelayed action may call for temporary departure from that normal balance of public procedure.

I am prepared under my constitutional duty to recommend the measures that a stricken Nation in the midst of a stricken world may require. These measures, or such other measures as the Congress may build out of its experience and wisdom, I shall seek, within my constitutional authority, to bring to speedy adoption.

But in the event that the Congress shall fail to take one of these two courses, and in the event that the national emergency is still critical, I shall not evade the clear course of duty that will then confront me. I shall ask the Congress for the one remaining instrument to meet the crisis — broad Executive power to wage a war against the emergency, as great as the power that would be given to me if we were in fact invaded by a foreign foe.

For the trust reposed in me I will return the courage and the devotion that befit the time. I can do no less.

We face the arduous days that lie before us in the warm courage of national unity; with the clear consciousness of seeking old and precious moral values; with the clean satisfaction that comes from the stern performance of duty by old and young alike. We aim at the assurance of a rounded and permanent national life.

We do not distrust the future of essential democracy. The people of the United States have not failed. In their need they have registered a mandate that they want direct, vigorous action. They have asked for discipline and direction under leadership. They have made me the present instrument of their wishes. In the spirit of the gift I take it.

In this dedication of a Nation we humbly ask the blessing of God. May He protect each and every one of us. May He guide me in the days to come.

Address at the Pan American Union

The Good Neighbor Policy

(April 12, 1933)

I rejoice in this opportunity to participate in the celebration of "Pan American Day" and to extend on behalf of the people of the United States a fraternal greeting to our sister American Republics. The celebration of "Pan American Day" in this building, dedicated to international good-will and cooperation, exemplifies a unity of thought and purpose among the peoples of this hemisphere. It is a manifestation of the common ideal of mutual helpfulness, sympathetic understanding and spiritual solidarity.

There is inspiration in the thought that on this day the attention of the citizens of the twenty-one Republics of America is focused on the common ties—historical, cultural, economic, and social—which bind them to one another. Common ideals and a community of interest, together with a spirit of cooperation, have led to the realization that the well-being of one Nation depends in large measure upon the well-being of its neighbors. It is upon these foundations that Pan Americanism has been built.

This celebration commemorates a movement based upon the policy of fraternal cooperation. In my Inaugural Address I stated that I would "dedicate this Nation to the policy of the good neighbor — the neighbor who resolutely respects himself and, because he does so, respects the rights of others — the neighbor who respects his obligations and respects the sanctity of his agreements in and with a world of neighbors." Never before has the significance of the words "good neighbor" been so manifest in international relations. Never have the need and benefit of neighborly cooperation in every form of human activity been so evident as they are today.

Friendship among Nations, as among individuals, calls for constructive efforts to muster the forces of humanity in order that an atmosphere of close understanding and cooperation may be cultivated. It involves mutual obligations and responsibilities, for it is only by sympathetic respect for the rights of others and a scrupulous fulfillment of the corresponding obligations by each member of the community that a true fraternity can be maintained.

The essential qualities of a true Pan Americanism must be the same as those which constitute a good neighbor, namely, mutual understanding, and, through such understanding, a sympathetic appreciation of the other's point of view. It is only in this manner that we can hope to build up a system of which confidence, friendship and good-will are the cornerstones.

In this spirit the people of every Republic on our continent are coming to a deep understanding of the fact that the Monroe Doctrine, of which so much has been written and spoken for more than a century was and is directed at the maintenance of independence by the peoples of the continent. It was aimed and is aimed against the acquisition in any manner of the control of additional territory in this hemisphere by any non-American power.

Hand in hand with this Pan American doctrine of continental self-defense, the peoples of the American Republics understand more clearly, with the passing years, that the independence of each Republic must recognize the independence of every other Republic. Each one of us must grow by an advancement of civilization and social well-being and not by the acquisition of territory at the expense of any neighbor.

In this spirit of mutual understanding and of cooperation on this continent you and I cannot fail to be disturbed by any armed strife between neighbors. I do not hesitate to say to you, the distinguished members of the Governing Board of the Pan American Union, that I regard existing conflicts between four of our sister Republics as a backward step.

Your Americanism and mine must be a structure built of confidence cemented by a sympathy which recognizes only equality and fraternity. It finds its source and being in the hearts of men and dwells in the temple of the intellect.

We all of us have peculiar problems, and, to speak frankly, the interest of our own citizens must, in each instance, come first. But it is equally true that it is of vital importance to every Nation of this Continent that the American Governments, individually, take, without further delay, such action as may be possible to abolish all unnecessary and artificial barriers and restrictions which now hamper the healthy flow of trade between the peoples of the American Republics.

I am glad to deliver this message to you, Gentlemen of the Governing Board of the Pan American Union, for I look upon the Union as the outward expression of the spiritual unity of the Americas. It is to this unity which must be courageous and vital in its element that humanity must look for one of the great stabilizing influences in world affairs.

In closing, may I refer to the ceremony which is to take place a little later in the morning at which the Government of Venezuela will present to the Pan American Union the bust of a great American leader and patriot, Francisco de Miranda. I join with you in this tribute.

Statement on Approval of the Neutrality Act of 1935

"To avoid any action which might involve us in war".

(August 31, 1935)

I have given my approval to S. J. Resolution 17, the neutrality legislation which passed the Congress last week.

I have approved this Joint Resolution because it was intended as an expression of the fixed desire of the Government and the people of the United States to avoid any action which might involve us in war. The purpose is wholly excellent, and this Joint Resolution will to a considerable degree serve that end.

It provides for a licensing system for the control of carrying arms, etc., by American vessels; for the control of the use of American waters by foreign submarines; for the restriction of travel by American citizens on vessels of belligerent Nations; and for the embargo of the export of arms, etc., to both belligerent Nations.

The latter Section terminates at the end of February, 1936. This Section requires further and more complete consideration between now and that date. Here again the objective is wholly good. It is the policy of this Government to avoid being drawn into wars between other Nations, but it is a fact that no Congress and no Executive can foresee all possible future situations. History is filled with unforeseeable situations that call for some flexibility of action. It is conceivable that situations may arise in which the wholly inflexible provisions of Section I of this Act might have exactly the opposite effect from that which was intended. In other words, the inflexible provisions might drag us into war instead of keeping us out. The policy of the Government is definitely committed to the maintenance of peace and the avoidance of any entanglements which would lead us into conflict. At the same time it is the policy of the Government by every peaceful means and without entanglement to cooperate with other similarly minded Governments to promote peace.

In several aspects further careful consideration of neutrality needs is most desirable and there can well be an expansion to include provisions dealing with other important aspects of our neutrality policy which have not been dealt with in this temporary measure.

Address on Armistice Day at Arlington Cemetery

"We must not hide our concern for grave world dangers".

(November 11, 1935)

Friends and fellow Americans:

The living memory of the World War is close to each and every one of us today. Our thoughts return to great objectives of the past, even as the minds of older men go back to their boyhood's ideals.

We Americans were so placed in those days that we gained a perspective of the great world conflict that was perhaps clearer than that of our fellow men who were closer to the scene of battle. For most of the first three years of the conflict we were not participants; but during the final phase we ourselves engaged on many fronts.

For that reason perhaps we understood, as well as any, the cries that went up—that the world conflict should be made a war to end wars. We were not invaded, nor were we threatened with invasion then or later; but the very distance of our view led us to perceive the dire results of war through days of following peace.

The primary purpose of the United States of America is to avoid being drawn into war. We seek also in every practicable way to promote peace and to discourage war. Except for those few who have placed or who place temporary, selfish gain ahead of national and world peace, the overwhelming mass of American citizens are in hearty accord with these basic policies of our Government, as they are also entirely sympathetic with the efforts of other Nations to avoid and to end war.

That is why we too have striven with great consistency to approve steps to remove the causes of war and to disapprove steps taken by others to commit acts of aggression. We have either led or performed our full part in every important attempt to limit and to reduce world armaments. We have sought by definite act and solemn commitment to establish the United States as a good neighbor among Nations. We are acting to simplify definitions and facts by calling war "War" when armed invasion and a resulting killing of human beings take place.

But though our course is consistent and clear, it is with disappointment and sorrow that most Americans confess that the world's gain thus far has been small.

I would not be frank with you if I did not tell you that the dangers that confront the future of mankind as a whole are greater to the world and therefore to us than the dangers which confront the people of the United States by and in themselves alone.

Jealousies between Nations continue; armaments increase; national ambitions that disturb the world's peace are thrust forward. Most serious of all, international confidence in the sacredness of international contracts is on the wane.

The memory of our hopes of 1917 and 1918 dies with the death of those of us who took part. It is, therefore, your sacred obligation and mine, by conscious, definite effort, to pass that memory on to succeeding generations. A new generation, even in its cradle or still unborn, is coming to the fore. The children in our schools, the young men and women passing through our colleges into productive life have, unlike us, no direct knowledge of the meaning of war. They are not immune to the glamour of war, to the opportunities to escape from the drabness and worry of hard times at home in the glory and heroism of the arms factory and the battlefield. Fortunately, there is evidence on every hand that the youth of America, as a whole, is not trapped by that delusion. They know that elation and prosperity which may come from a new war must lead — for those who survive it — to economic and social collapse more sweeping than any we have experienced in the past. While, therefore, we cannot and must not hide our concern for grave world dangers, and while, at the same time, we cannot and must not build walls around ourselves and hide our heads in the sand, we must go forward with all our strength to stress and strive for international peace.

In this effort America must and will protect herself. Under no circumstances will this policy of self-protection go to lengths beyond self-protection. Aggression on the part of the United States is an impossibility in so far as the present Administration of your Government is concerned. Defense against aggression by others — adequate defense on land, on sea and in air — is our accepted policy; and the measure of that defense is and will be solely the amount necessary to safeguard us against the armaments of others. The more greatly they decrease their armaments, the more quickly and surely shall we decrease ours.

In many other fields, by word and by deed, we are giving example to the world by removing or lowering barriers which impede friendly intercourse. Our soldier and sailor dead call to us across the years to make our lives effective in building constructively for peace. It is fitting that on this Armistice Day, seventeen years later, I am privileged to tell you that between us and a great neighbor another act cementing our historic friendship has been agreed upon and is being consummated. Between Canada and the United States exists a neighborliness, a genuine friendship which for over a century has dispelled every passing rift.

Our two peoples, each independent, are closely knit by ties of blood and a common heritage; our standards of life are substantially the same; our commerce and our economic conditions rest upon the same foundations. Between two such peoples, if we would build constructively for peace and progress, the flow of intercourse should be mutually beneficial and not unduly hampered. Each has much to gain by material profit, by spiritual profit, by increased employment through the means of enlarged trade, one with the other.

I am, therefore, happy to be able to tell you almost in celebration of this Armistice Day that the Canadian Prime Minister and I, after thoughtful discussion of our national problems, have reached a definite agreement which will eliminate disagreements and unreasonable restrictions, and thus work to the advantage of both Canada and the United States.

I hope that this good example will reach around the world some day, for the power of good example is the strongest force in the world. It surpasses preachments; it excels good resolutions; it is far better than agreements unfulfilled.

If we as a Nation, by our good example, can contribute to the peaceful well-being of the fellowship of Nations, our course through the years will not have been in vain.

We who survive have profited by the good example of our fellow Americans who gave their lives in war. On these surrounding hills of Virginia they rest—thousands upon thousands—in the last bivouac of the dead. Below us, across the river, we see a great capital of a great Nation.

The past and the present unite in prayer that America will ever seek the ways of peace, and by her example at home and abroad speed the return of good-will among men.

Acceptance Speech at the Democratic National Convention

"The royalists of the economic order".

(June 27, 1936)

Senator Robinson, Members of the Democratic Convention, my friends:

Here, and in every community throughout the land, we are met at a time of great moment to the future of the Nation. It is an occasion to be dedicated to the simple and sincere expression of an attitude toward problems, the determination of which will profoundly affect America.

I come not only as a leader of a party, not only as a candidate for high office, but as one upon whom many critical hours have imposed and still impose a grave responsibility.

For the sympathy, help and confidence with which Americans have sustained me in my task I am grateful. For their loyalty I salute the members of our great party, in and out of political life in every part of the Union. I salute those of other parties, especially those in the Congress of the United States who on so many occasions have put partisanship aside. I thank the Governors of the several States, their Legislatures, their State and local officials who participated unselfishly and regardless of party in our efforts to achieve recovery and destroy abuses. Above all I thank the millions of Americans who have borne disaster bravely and have dared to smile through the storm.

America will not forget these recent years, will not forget that the rescue was not a mere party task. It was the concern of all of us. In our strength we rose together, rallied our energies together, applied the old rules of common sense, and together survived.

In those days we feared fear. That was why we fought fear. And today, my friends, we have won against the most dangerous of our foes. We have conquered fear.

But I cannot, with candor, tell you that all is well with the world. Clouds of suspicion, tides of ill-will and intolerance gather darkly in many places. In our own land we enjoy indeed a fullness of life greater than that of most Nations. But the rush of modern civilization itself has raised for us new difficulties, new problems which must be solved if we are to preserve to the United States the political and economic freedom for which Washington and Jefferson planned and fought.

Philadelphia is a good city in which to write American history. This is fitting ground on which to reaffirm the faith of our fathers; to pledge ourselves to restore to the people a wider freedom; to give to 1936 as the founders gave to 1776 — an American way of life.

That very word freedom, in itself and of necessity, suggests freedom from some restraining power. In 1776 we sought freedom from the tyranny of a political autocracy — from the eighteenth century royalists who held special privileges from the crown. It was to perpetuate their privilege that they governed without the consent of the governed; that they denied the right of free assembly and free speech; that they restricted the worship of God; that they put the average man's property and the average man's life in pawn to the mercenaries of dynastic power; that they regimented the people.

And so it was to win freedom from the tyranny of political autocracy that the American Revolution was fought. That victory gave the business of governing into the hands of the average man, who won the right with his neighbors to make and order his own destiny through his own Government. Political tyranny was wiped out at Philadelphia on July 4, 1776.

Since that struggle, however, man's inventive genius released new forces in our land which reordered the lives of our people. The age of machinery, of railroads; of steam and electricity; the telegraph and the radio; mass production, mass distribution—all of these combined to bring forward a new civilization and with it a new problem for those who sought to remain free.

For out of this modern civilization economic royalists carved new dynasties. New kingdoms were built upon concentration of control over material things. Through new uses of corporations, banks and securities, new machinery of industry and agriculture, of labor and capital—all undreamed of by the fathers—the whole structure of modern life was impressed into this royal service.

There was no place among this royalty for our many thousands of small business men and merchants who sought to make a worthy use of the American system of initiative and profit. They were no more free than the worker or the farmer. Even honest and progressive-minded men of wealth, aware of their obligation to their generation, could never know just where they fitted into this dynastic scheme of things.

It was natural and perhaps human that the privileged princes of these new economic dynasties, thirsting for power, reached out for control over Government itself. They created a new despotism and wrapped it in the robes of legal sanction. In its service new mercenaries sought to regiment the people, their labor, and their property. And as a result the average man once more confronts the problem that faced the Minute Man.

The hours men and women worked, the wages they received, the conditions of their labor—these had passed beyond the control of the people, and were imposed by this new industrial dictatorship. The savings of the average family, the capital of the small business man, the investments set aside for old age—other people's money—these were tools which the new economic royalty used to dig itself in.

Those who tilled the soil no longer reaped the rewards which were their right. The small measure of their gains was decreed by men in distant cities.

Throughout the Nation, opportunity was limited by monopoly. Individual initiative was crushed in the cogs of a great machine. The field open for free business was more and more restricted. Private enterprise, indeed, became too private. It became privileged enterprise, not free enterprise.

An old English judge once said: "Necessitous men are not free men." Liberty requires opportunity to make a living—a living decent according to the standard of the time, a living which gives man not only enough to live by, but something to live for.

For too many of us the political equality we once had won was meaningless in the face of economic inequality. A small group had concentrated into their own hands an almost complete control over other people's property, other people's money, other people's labor, other people's lives. For too many of us life was no longer free; liberty no longer real; men could no longer follow the pursuit of happiness.

Against economic tyranny such as this, the American citizen could appeal only to the organized power of Government. The collapse of 1929 showed up the despotism for what it was. The election of 1932 was the people's mandate to end it. Under that mandate it is being ended.

The royalists of the economic order have conceded that political freedom was the business of the Government, but they have maintained that economic slavery was nobody's business. They granted that the Government could protect the citizen in his right to vote, but they denied that the Government could do anything to protect the citizen in his right to work and his right to live.

Today we stand committed to the proposition that freedom is no half-and-half affair. If the average citizen is guaranteed equal opportunity in the polling place, he must have equal opportunity in the market place.

These economic royalists complain that we seek to overthrow the institutions of America. What they really complain of is that we seek to take away their power. Our allegiance to American institutions requires the overthrow of this kind of power. In vain they seek to hide behind the Flag and the Constitution. In their blindness they forget what the Flag and the Constitution stand for. Now, as always, they stand for democracy, not tyranny; for freedom, not subjection; and against a dictatorship by mob rule and the over-privileged alike.

The brave and clear platform adopted by this Convention, to which I heartily subscribe, sets forth that Government in a modern civilization has certain inescapable obligations to its citizens, among which are protection of the family and the home, the establishment of a democracy of opportunity, and aid to those overtaken by disaster.

But the resolute enemy within our gates is ever ready to beat down our words unless in greater courage we will fight for them.

For more than three years we have fought for them. This Convention, in every word and deed, has pledged that that fight will go on.

The defeats and victories of these years have given to us as a people a new understanding of our Government and of ourselves. Never since the early days of the New England town meeting have the affairs of Government been so widely discussed and so clearly appreciated. It has been brought home to us that the only effective guide for the safety of this most worldly of worlds, the greatest guide of all, is moral principle.

We do not see faith, hope and charity as unattainable ideals, but we use them as stout supports of a Nation fighting the fight for freedom in a modern civilization.

Faith—in the soundness of democracy in the midst of dictatorships.

Hope—renewed because we know so well the progress we have made.

Charity—in the true spirit of that grand old word. For charity literally translated from the original means love, the love that understands, that does not merely share the wealth of the giver, but in true sympathy and wisdom helps men to help themselves.

We seek not merely to make Government a mechanical implement, but to give it the vibrant personal character that is the very embodiment of human charity.

We are poor indeed if this Nation cannot afford to lift from every recess of American life the dread fear of the unemployed that they are not needed in the world. We cannot afford to accumulate a deficit in the books of human fortitude.

In the place of the palace of privilege we seek to build a temple out of faith and hope and charity.

It is a sobering thing, my friends, to be a servant of this great cause. We try in our daily work to remember that the cause belongs not to us, but to the people. The standard is not in the hands of you and me alone. It is carried by America. We seek daily to profit from experience, to learn to do better as our task proceeds.

Governments can err, Presidents do make mistakes, but the immortal Dante tells us that divine justice weighs the sins of the cold-blooded and the sins of the warm-hearted in different scales.

Better the occasional faults of a Government that lives in a spirit of charity than the consistent omissions of a Government frozen in the ice of its own indifference.

There is a mysterious cycle in human events. To some generations much is given. Of other generations much is expected. This generation of Americans has a rendezvous with destiny.

In this world of ours in other lands, there are some people, who, in times past, have lived and fought for freedom, and seem to have grown too weary to carry on the fight. They have sold their heritage of freedom for the illusion of a living. They have yielded their democracy.

I believe in my heart that only our success can stir their ancient hope. They begin to know that here in America we are waging a great and successful war. It is not alone a war against want and destitution and economic demoralization. It is more than that; it is a war for the survival of democracy. We are fighting to save a great and precious form of government for ourselves and for the world.

I accept the commission you have tendered me. I join with you. I am enlisted for the duration of the war.

Address at Chautauqua, New York

"I hate war"

(August 14, 1936)

As many of you who are here tonight know, I formed the excellent habit of coming to Chautauqua more than twenty years ago. After my Inauguration in 1933, I promised Mr. Bestor that during the next four years I would come to Chautauqua again. It is in fulfillment of this that I am with you tonight.

A few days ago I was asked what the subject of this talk would be; and I replied that for two good reasons I wanted to discuss the subject of peace: First, because it is eminently appropriate in Chautauqua and, second, because in the hurly-burly of domestic politics it is important that our people should not overlook problems and issues which, though they lie beyond our borders, may, and probably will, have a vital influence on the United States of the future.

Many who have visited me in Washington in the past few months may have been surprised when I have told them that personally and because of my own daily contacts with all manner of difficult situations I am more concerned and less cheerful about international world conditions than about our immediate domestic prospects.

I say this to you not as a confirmed pessimist but as one who still hopes that envy, hatred and malice among Nations have reached their peak and will be succeeded by a new tide of peace and good-will. I say this as one who has participated in many of the decisions of peace and war before, during and after the World War; one who has traveled much; and one who has spent a goodly portion of every twenty-four hours in the study of foreign relations.

Long before I returned to Washington as President of the United States, I had made up my mind that pending what might be called a more opportune moment on other continents, the United States could best serve the cause of a peaceful humanity by setting an example. That was why on the 4th of March, 1933, I made the following declaration:

"In the field of world policy I would dedicate this Nation to the policy of the good neighbor—the neighbor who resolutely respects himself and, because he does so, respects the rights of others—the neighbor who respects his obligations and respects the sanctity of his agreements in and with a world of neighbors."

This declaration represents my purpose; but it represents more than a purpose, for it stands for a practice. To a measurable degree it has succeeded; the whole world now knows that the United States cherishes no predatory ambitions. We are strong; but less powerful Nations know that they need not fear our strength. We seek no conquests; we stand for peace.

In the whole of the Western Hemisphere our good-neighbor policy has produced results that are especially heartening.

The noblest monument to peace and to neighborly economic and I social friendship in all the world is not a monument in bronze or stone, but the boundary which unites the United States and Canada—3,000 miles of friendship with no barbed wire, no gun or soldier, and no passport on the whole frontier.

Mutual trust made that frontier. To extend the same sort of mutual trust throughout the Americas was our aim.

The American Republics to the south of us have been ready always to cooperate with the United States on a basis of equality and mutual respect, but before we inaugurated the good-neighbor policy there were among them resentment and fear, because certain Administrations in Washington had slighted their national pride and their sovereign rights.

In pursuance of the good-neighbor policy, and because in my younger days I had learned many lessons in the hard school of experience, I stated that the United States was opposed definitely to armed intervention.

We have negotiated a Pan American convention embodying the principle of non-intervention. We have abandoned the Platt Amendment which gave us the right to intervene in the internal affairs of the Republic of Cuba. We have withdrawn American marines from Haiti. We have signed a new treaty which places our relations with Panama on a mutually satisfactory basis. We have undertaken a series of trade agreements with other American countries to our mutual commercial profit. At the request of two neighboring Republics, I hope to give assistance in the final settlement of the last serious boundary dispute between any of the American Nations.

Throughout the Americas the spirit of the good neighbor is a practical and living fact. The twenty-one American Republics are not only living together in friendship and in peace; they are united in the determination so to remain.

To give substance to this determination a conference will meet on December 1, 1936, at the capital of our great Southern neighbor, Argentina, and it is, I know, the hope of all Chiefs of State of the Americas that this will result in measures which will banish wars forever from this vast portion of the earth.

Peace, like charity, begins at home; that is why we have begun at home. But peace in the Western world is not all that we seek.

It is our hope that knowledge of the practical application of the good-neighbor policy in this hemisphere will be borne home to our neighbors across the seas.

For ourselves we are on good terms with them—terms in most cases of straightforward friendship, of peaceful understanding.

But, of necessity, we are deeply concerned about tendencies of recent years among many of the Nations of other continents. It is a bitter experience to us when the spirit of agreements to which we are a party is not lived up to. It is an even more bitter experience for the whole company of Nations to witness not only the spirit but the letter of international agreements violated with impunity and without regard to the simple principles of honor. Permanent friendships between Nations as between men can be sustained only by scrupulous respect for the pledged word.

In spite of all this we have sought steadfastly to assist international movements to prevent war. We cooperated to the bitter end—and it was a bitter end—in the work of the General Disarmament Conference. When it failed we sought a separate treaty to deal with the manufacture of arms and the international traffic in arms. That proposal also came to nothing. We participated—again to the bitter end—in a conference to continue naval limitations, and when it became evident that no general treaty could be signed because of the objections of other Nations, we concluded with Great Britain and France a conditional treaty of qualitative limitation which, much to my regret, already shows signs of ineffectiveness.

We shun political commitments which might entangle us in foreign wars; we avoid connection with the political activities of the League of Nations; but I am glad to say that we have cooperated wholeheartedly in the social and humanitarian work at Geneva. Thus we are a part of the world effort to control traffic in narcotics, to improve international health, to help child welfare, to eliminate double taxation and to better working conditions and laboring hours throughout the world.

We are not isolationists except in so far as we seek to isolate ourselves completely from war. Yet we must remember that so long as war exists on earth there will be some danger that even the Nation which most ardently desires peace may be drawn into war.

I have seen war. I have seen war on land and sea. I have seen blood running from the wounded. I have seen men coughing out their gassed lungs. I have seen the dead in the mud. I have seen cities destroyed. I have seen two hundred limping exhausted men come out of line — the survivors of a regiment of one thousand that went forward forty-eight hours before. I have seen children starving. I have seen the agony of mothers and wives. I hate war.

I have passed unnumbered hours, I shall pass unnumbered hours, thinking and planning how war may be kept from this Nation.

I wish I could keep war from all Nations; but that is beyond my power. I can at least make certain that no act of the United States helps to produce or to promote war. I can at least make clear that the conscience of America revolts against war and that any Nation which provokes war forfeits the sympathy of the people of the United States.

Many causes produce war. There are ancient hatreds, turbulent frontiers, the "legacy of old forgotten, far-off things, and battles long ago." There are new-born fanaticisms. Convictions on the part of certain peoples that they have become the unique depositories of ultimate truth and right.

A dark old world was devastated by wars between conflicting religions. A dark modern world faces wars between conflicting economic and political fanaticisms in which are intertwined race hatreds. To bring it home, it is as if within the territorial limits of the United States, forty-eight Nations with forty-eight forms of government, forty-eight customs barriers, forty-eight languages, and forty-eight eternal and different verities, were spending their time and their substance in a frenzy of effort to make themselves strong enough to conquer their neighbors or strong enough to defend themselves against their neighbors.

In one field, that of economic barriers, the American policy may be, I hope, of some assistance in discouraging the economic source of war and therefore a contribution toward the peace of the world. The trade agreements which we are making are not only finding outlets for the products of American fields and American factories but are also pointing the way to the elimination of embargoes, quotas and other devices which place such pressure on Nations not possessing great natural resources that to them the price of peace seems less terrible than the price of war.

We do not maintain that a more liberal international trade will stop war; but we fear that without a more liberal international trade, war is a natural sequence.

The Congress of the United States has given me certain authority to provide safeguards of American neutrality in case of war.

The President of the United States, who, under our Constitution, is vested with primary authority to conduct our international relations, thus has been given new weapons with which to maintain our neutrality.

Nevertheless—and I speak from a long experience—the effective maintenance of American neutrality depends today, as in the past, on the wisdom and determination of whoever at the moment occupy the offices of President and Secretary of State.

It is clear that our present policy and the measures passed by the Congress would, in the event of a war on some other continent, reduce war profits which would otherwise accrue to American citizens. Industrial and agricultural production for a war market may give immense fortunes to a few men; for the Nation as a whole it produces disaster. It was the prospect of war profits that made our farmers in the West plow up prairie land that should never have been plowed, but should have been left for grazing cattle. Today we are reaping the harvest of those war profits in the dust storms which have devastated those war-plowed areas.

It was the prospect of war profits that caused the extension of monopoly and unjustified expansion of industry and a price level so high that the normal relationship between debtor and creditor was destroyed.

Nevertheless, if war should break out again in another continent, let us not blink the fact that we would find in this country thousands of Americans who, seeking immediate riches — fools' gold — would attempt to break down or evade our neutrality.

They would tell you — and, unfortunately, their views would get wide publicity — that if they could produce and ship this and that and the other article to belligerent Nations, the unemployed of America would all find work. They would tell you that if they could extend credit to warring Nations that credit would be used in the United States to build homes and factories and pay our debts. They would tell you that America once more would capture the trade of the world.

It would be hard to resist that clamor; it would be hard for many Americans, I fear, to look beyond — to realize the inevitable penalties, the inevitable day of reckoning, that come from a false prosperity.

To resist the clamor of that greed, if war should come, would require the unswerving support of all Americans who love peace.

If we face the choice of profits or peace, the Nation will answer — must answer — "We choose peace." It is the duty of all of us to encourage such a body of public opinion in this country that the answer will be clear and for all practical purposes unanimous.

With that wise and experienced man who is our Secretary of State, whose statesmanship has met with such wide approval, I have thought and worked long and hard on the problem of keeping the United States at peace. But all the wisdom of America is not to be found in the White House or in the Department of State; we need the meditation, the prayer, and the positive support of the people of America who go along with us in seeking peace.

No matter how well we are supported by neutrality legislation, we must remember that no laws can be provided to cover every contingency, for it is impossible to imagine how every future event may shape itself. In spite of every possible forethought, international relations involve of necessity a vast uncharted area. In that area safe sailing will depend on the knowledge and the experience and the wisdom of those who direct our foreign policy. Peace will depend on their day-to-day decisions.

At this late date, with the wisdom which is so easy after the event and so difficult before the event, we find it possible to trace the tragic series of small decisions which led Europe into the Great War in 1914 and eventually engulfed us and many other Nations.

We can keep out of war if those who watch and decide have a sufficiently detailed understanding of international affairs to make certain that the small decisions of each day do not lead toward war and if, at the same time, they possess the courage to say "no" to those who selfishly or unwisely would let us go to war.

Of all the Nations of the world today we are in many ways most singularly blessed. Our closest neighbors are good neighbors. If there are remoter Nations that wish us not good but ill, they know that we are strong; they know that we can and will defend ourselves and defend our neighborhood.

We seek to dominate no other Nation. We ask no territorial expansion. We oppose imperialism. We desire reduction in world armaments.

We believe in democracy; we believe in freedom; we believe in peace. We offer to every Nation of the world the handclasp of the good neighbor. Let those who wish our friendship look us in the eye and take our hand.

Speech at Madison Square Garden

"I welcome their hatred"

(October 31, 1936)

Senator Wagner, Governor Lehman, ladies and gentlemen:

On the eve of a national election, it is well for us to stop for a moment and analyze calmly and without prejudice the effect on our Nation of a victory by either of the major political parties.

The problem of the electorate is far deeper, far more vital than the continuance in the Presidency of any individual. For the greater issue goes beyond units of humanity — it goes to humanity itself.

In 1932 the issue was the restoration of American democracy; and the American people were in a mood to win. They did win. In 1936 the issue is the preservation of their victory. Again they are in a mood to win. Again they will win.

More than four years ago in accepting the Democratic nomination in Chicago, I said: "Give me your help not to win votes alone, but to win in this crusade to restore America to its own people."

The banners of that crusade still fly in the van of a Nation that is on the march.

It is needless to repeat the details of the program which this Administration has been hammering out on the anvils of experience. No amount of misrepresentation or statistical contortion can conceal or blur or smear that record. Neither the attacks of unscrupulous enemies nor the exaggerations of over-zealous friends will serve to mislead the American people.

What was our hope in 1932? Above all other things the American people wanted peace. They wanted peace of mind instead of gnawing fear.

First, they sought escape from the personal terror which had stalked them for three years. They wanted the peace that comes from security in their homes: safety for their savings, permanence in their jobs, a fair profit from their enterprise.

Next, they wanted peace in the community, the peace that springs from the ability to meet the needs of community life: schools, playgrounds, parks, sanitation, highways — those things which are expected of solvent local government. They sought escape from disintegration and bankruptcy in local and state affairs.

They also sought peace within the Nation: protection of their currency, fairer wages, the ending of long hours of toil, the abolition of child labor, the elimination of wild-cat speculation, the safety of their children from kidnappers.

And, finally, they sought peace with other Nations — peace in a world of unrest. The Nation knows that I hate war, and I know that the Nation hates war.

I submit to you a record of peace; and on that record a well-founded expectation for future peace — peace for the individual, peace for the community, peace for the Nation, and peace with the world.

Tonight I call the roll—the roll of honor of those who stood with us in 1932 and still stand with us today.

Written on it are the names of millions who never had a chance—men at starvation wages, women in sweatshops, children at looms.

Written on it are the names of those who despaired, young men and young women for whom opportunity had become a will-o'-the-wisp.

Written on it are the names of farmers whose acres yielded only bitterness, business men whose books were portents of disaster, home owners who were faced with eviction, frugal citizens whose savings were insecure.

Written there in large letters are the names of countless other Americans of all parties and all faiths, Americans who had eyes to see and hearts to understand, whose consciences were burdened because too many of their fellows were burdened, who looked on these things four years ago and said, "This can be changed. We will change it."

We still lead that army in 1936. They stood with us then because in 1932 they believed. They stand with us today because in 1936 they know. And with them stand millions of new recruits who have come to know.

Their hopes have become our record.

We have not come this far without a struggle and I assure you we cannot go further without a struggle.

For twelve years this Nation was afflicted with hear-nothing, see-nothing, do-nothing Government. The Nation looked to Government but the Government looked away. Nine mocking years with the golden calf and three long years of the scourge! Nine crazy years at the ticker and three long years in the breadlines! Nine mad years of mirage and three long years of despair! Powerful influences strive today to restore that kind of government with its doctrine that that Government is best which is most indifferent.

For nearly four years you have had an Administration which instead of twirling its thumbs has rolled up its sleeves. We will keep our sleeves rolled up.

We had to struggle with the old enemies of peace—business and financial monopoly, speculation, reckless banking, class antagonism, sectionalism, war profiteering.

They had begun to consider the Government of the United States as a mere appendage to their own affairs. We know now that Government by organized money is just as dangerous as Government by organized mob.

Never before in all our history have these forces been so united against one candidate as they stand today. They are unanimous in their hate for me—and I welcome their hatred.

I should like to have it said of my first Administration that in it the forces of selfishness and of lust for power met their match. I should like to have it said of my second Administration that in it these forces met their master.

The American people know from a four-year record that today there is only one entrance to the White House—by the front door. Since March 4, 1933, there has been only one pass-key to the White House. I have carried that key in my pocket. It is there tonight. So long as I am President, it will remain in my pocket.

Those who used to have pass-keys are not happy. Some of them are desperate. Only desperate men with their backs to the wall would descend so far below the level of decent citizenship as to foster the current pay-envelope campaign against America's working people. Only reckless men, heedless of consequences, would risk the disruption of the hope for a new peace between worker and employer by returning to the tactics of the labor spy.

Here is an amazing paradox! The very employers and politicians and publishers who talk most loudly of class antagonism and the destruction of the American system now undermine that system by this attempt to coerce the votes of the wage earners of this country. It is the 1936 version of the old threat to close down the factory or the office if a particular candidate does not win. It is an old strategy of tyrants to delude their victims into fighting their battles for them.

Every message in a pay envelope, even if it is the truth, is a command to vote according to the will of the employer. But this propaganda is worse — it is deceit.

They tell the worker his wage will be reduced by a contribution to some vague form of old-age insurance. They carefully conceal from him the fact that for every dollar of premium he pays for that insurance, the employer pays another dollar. That omission is deceit.

They carefully conceal from him the fact that under the federal law, he receives another insurance policy to help him if he loses his job, and that the premium of that policy is paid 100 percent by the employer and not one cent by the worker. They do not tell him that the insurance policy that is bought for him is far more favorable to him than any policy that any private insurance company could afford to issue. That omission is deceit.

They imply to him that he pays all the cost of both forms of insurance. They carefully conceal from him the fact that for every dollar put up by him his employer puts up three dollars three for one. And that omission is deceit.

But they are guilty of more than deceit. When they imply that the reserves thus created against both these policies will be stolen by some future Congress, diverted to some wholly foreign purpose, they attack the integrity and honor of American Government itself. Those who suggest that, are already aliens to the spirit of American democracy. Let them emigrate and try their lot under some foreign flag in which they have more confidence.

The fraudulent nature of this attempt is well shown by the record of votes on the passage of the Social Security Act. In addition to an overwhelming majority of Democrats in both

Houses, seventy-seven Republican Representatives voted for it and only eighteen against it and fifteen Republican Senators voted for it and only five against it. Where does this last-minute drive of the Republican leadership leave these Republican Representatives and Senators who helped enact this law?

I am sure the vast majority of law-abiding businessmen who are not parties to this propaganda fully appreciate the extent of the threat to honest business contained in this coercion.

I have expressed indignation at this form of campaigning and I am confident that the overwhelming majority of employers, workers and the general public share that indignation and will show it at the polls on Tuesday next.

Aside from this phase of it, I prefer to remember this campaign not as bitter but only as hard-fought. There should be no bitterness or hate where the sole thought is the welfare of the United States of America. No man can occupy the office of President without realizing that he is President of all the people.

It is because I have sought to think in terms of the whole Nation that I am confident that today, just as four years ago, the people want more than promises.

Our vision for the future contains more than promises.

This is our answer to those who, silent about their own plans, ask us to state our objectives.

Of course we will continue to seek to improve working conditions for the workers of America — to reduce hours over-long, to increase wages that spell starvation, to end the labor of children, to wipe out sweatshops. Of course we will continue every effort to end monopoly in business, to support collective bargaining, to stop unfair competition, to abolish dishonorable trade practices. For all these we have only just begun to fight.

Of course we will continue to work for cheaper electricity in the homes and on the farms of America, for better and cheaper transportation, for low interest rates, for sounder home financing, for better banking, for the regulation of security issues, for reciprocal trade among nations, for the wiping out of slums. For all these we have only just begun to fight.

Of course we will continue our efforts in behalf of the farmers of America. With their continued cooperation we will do all in our power to end the piling up of huge surpluses which spelled ruinous prices for their crops. We will persist in successful action for better land use, for reforestation, for the conservation of water all the way from its source to the sea, for drought and flood control, for better marketing facilities for farm commodities, for a definite reduction of farm tenancy, for encouragement of farmer cooperatives, for crop insurance and a stable food supply. For all these we have only just begun to fight.

Of course we will provide useful work for the needy unemployed; we prefer useful work to the pauperism of a dole.

Here and now I want to make myself clear about those who disparage their fellow citizens on the relief rolls. They say that those on relief are not merely jobless — that they are worthless. Their solution for the relief problem is to end relief — to purge the rolls by starvation. To use the language of the stock broker, our needy unemployed would be cared for when, as, and if some fairy godmother should happen on the scene.

You and I will continue to refuse to accept that estimate of our unemployed fellow Americans. Your Government is still on the same side of the street with the Good Samaritan and not with those who pass by on the other side.

Again — what of our objectives?

Of course we will continue our efforts for young men and women so that they may obtain an education and an opportunity to put it to use. Of course we will continue our help for the crippled, for the blind, for the mothers, our insurance for the unemployed, our security for the aged. Of course we will continue to protect the consumer against unnecessary price spreads, against the costs that are added by monopoly and speculation. We will continue our successful efforts to increase his purchasing power and to keep it constant.

For these things, too, and for a multitude of others like them, we have only just begun to fight.

All this—all these objectives—spell peace at home. All our actions, all our ideals, spell also peace with other nations.

Today there is war and rumor of war. We want none of it. But while we guard our shores against threats of war, we will continue to remove the causes of unrest and antagonism at home which might make our people easier victims to those for whom foreign war is profitable. You know well that those who stand to profit by war are not on our side in this campaign.

"Peace on earth, good will toward men"—democracy must cling to that message. For it is my deep conviction that democracy cannot live without that true religion which gives a nation a sense of justice and of moral purpose. Above our political forums, above our market places stand the altars of our faith—altars on which burn the fires of devotion that maintain all that is best in us and all that is best in our Nation.

We have need of that devotion today. It is that which makes it possible for government to persuade those who are mentally prepared to fight each other to go on instead, to work for and to sacrifice for each other. That is why we need to say with the Prophet: "What doth the Lord require of thee—but to do justly, to love mercy and to walk humbly with thy God." That is why the recovery we seek, the recovery we are winning, is more than economic. In it are included justice and love and humility, not for ourselves as individuals alone, but for our Nation.

That is the road to peace.

Address before the Inter-American Conference for the Maintenance of Peace

"More than the mere clash of armies."

(December 1, 1936)

Members of the American Family of Nations:

On the happy occasion of the convening of this Conference I address you thus, because members of a family need no introduction or formalities when, in pursuance of excellent custom, they meet together for their common good.

As a family we appreciate the hospitality of our host, President Justo, and the Government and people of Argentina; and all of us are happy that to our friend Dr. Saavedra Lamas has come the well deserved award of the Nobel Prize for great service in the cause of world peace.

Three years ago the American family met in nearby Montevideo, the great capital of the Republic of Uruguay. They were dark days. A shattering depression, unparalleled in its intensity, held us, with the rest of the world, in its grip. And in our own Hemisphere a tragic war was raging between two of our sister Republics.

Yet, at that conference there was born not only hope for our common future but a greater measure of mutual trust between the American democracies than had ever existed before. In this Western Hemisphere the night of fear has been dispelled. Many of the intolerable burdens of economic depression have been lightened and, due in no small part to our common efforts, every Nation of this Hemisphere is today at peace with its neighbors.

This is no conference to form alliances, to divide the spoils of war, to partition countries, to deal with human beings as though they were pawns in a game of chance. Our purpose, under happy auspices, is to assure the continuance of the blessings of peace.

Three years ago, recognizing that a crisis was being thrust upon the New World, with splendid unanimity our twenty-one Republics set an example to the whole world by proclaiming a new spirit, a new day, in the affairs of this Hemisphere.

While the succeeding period has justified in full measure all that was said and done at Montevideo, it has unfortunately emphasized the seriousness of threats to peace among other Nations. Events elsewhere have served only to strengthen our horror of war and all that war means. The men, women, and children of the Americas know that warfare in this day and age means more than the mere clash of armies: they see the destruction of cities and of farms; they foresee that children and grandchildren, if they survive, will stagger for long years not only under the burden of poverty but also amid the threat of broken society and the destruction of constitutional government.

I am profoundly convinced that the plain people everywhere in the civilized world today wish to live in peace one with another. And still leaders and Governments resort to war. Truly, if the genius of mankind that has invented the weapons of death cannot discover the means of preserving peace, civilization as we know it lives in an evil day.

But we cannot now, especially in view of our common purpose, accept any defeatist attitude. We have learned by hard experience that peace is not to be had for the mere asking; that peace, like other great privileges, can be obtained only by hard and painstaking effort. We are here to dedicate ourselves and our countries to that work.

You who assemble today carry with you in your deliberations the hopes of millions of human beings in other less fortunate lands. Beyond the ocean we see continents rent asunder by old hatreds and new fanaticisms. We hear the demand that injustice and inequality be corrected by resorting to the sword and not by resorting to reason and peaceful justice. We hear the cry that new markets can be achieved only through conquest. We read that the sanctity of treaties between Nations is disregarded.

We know, too, that vast armaments are rising on every side and that the work of creating them employs men and women by the millions. It is natural, however, for us to conclude that such employment is false employment; that it builds no permanent structures and creates no consumers' goods for the maintenance of a lasting prosperity. We know that Nations guilty of these follies inevitably face the day when either their weapons of destruction must be used against their neighbors or when an unsound economy, like a house of cards, will fall apart.

In either case, even though the Americas become involved in no war, we must suffer too. The madness of a great war in other parts of the world would affect us and threaten our good in a hundred ways. And the economic collapse of any Nation or Nations must of necessity arm our own prosperity.

Can we, the Republics of the New World, help the Old World to avert the catastrophe which impends? Yes; I am confident that we can.

First, it is our duty by every honorable means to prevent any future war among ourselves. This can best be done through the strengthening of the processes of constitutional democratic government; by making these processes conform to the modern need for unity and efficiency and, at the same time, preserving the individual liberties of our citizens. By so doing, the people of our Nations, unlike the people of many Nations who live under other forms of governments can and will insist on their intention to live in peace. Thus will democratic government be justified throughout the world.

In this determination to live at peace among ourselves we in the Americas make it at the same time clear that we stand shoulder to shoulder in our final determination that others who, driven by war madness or land hunger, might seek to commit acts of aggression against us will find a Hemisphere wholly prepared to consult together for our mutual safety and our mutual good. I repeat what I said in speaking before the Congress and the Supreme Court of Brazil: "Each one of us has learned the glories of independence. Let each one of us learn the glories of interdependence."

Secondly, and in addition to the perfecting of the mechanisms of peace, we can strive even more strongly than in the past to prevent the creation of those conditions which give rise to war. Lack of social or political justice within the borders of any Nation is always cause for concern. Through democratic processes we can strive to achieve for the Americas the highest possible standard of living conditions for all our people. Men and women blessed with political freedom, willing to work and able to find work, rich enough to maintain their families and to educate their children, contented with their lot in life and on terms of friendship with their neighbors, will defend themselves to the utmost, but will never consent to take up arms for a war of conquest.

Interwoven with these problems is the further self-evident fact that the welfare and prosperity of each of our Nations depend in large part on the benefits derived from commerce among ourselves and with other Nations, for our present civilization rests on the basis of an international exchange of commodities. Every Nation of the world has felt the evil effects of recent efforts to erect trade barriers of every known kind. Every individual citizen has suffered from them. It is no accident that the Nations which have carried this process farthest are those which proclaim most loudly that they require war as an instrument of their policy. It is no accident that attempts to be self-sufficient have led to falling standards for their people and to ever-increasing loss of the democratic ideals in a mad race to pile armament on armament. It is no accident that, because of these suicidal policies and the suffering attending them, many of their people have come to believe with despair that the price of war seems less than the price of peace.

This state of affairs we must refuse to accept with every instinct of defense, with every exhortation of enthusiastic hope, with every use of mind and skill.

I cannot refrain here from reiterating my gratification that in this, as in so many other achievements, the American Republics have given a salutary example to the world. The resolution adopted at the Inter-American Conference at Montevideo endorsing the principles of liberal trade policies has shone forth like a beacon in the storm of economic madness which has been sweeping over the entire world during these later years. Truly, if the principles there embodied find still wider application in your deliberations, it will be a notable contribution to the cause of peace. For my own part I have done all in my power to sustain the consistent efforts of my Secretary of State in negotiating agreements for reciprocal trade, and even though the individual results may seem small, the total of them is significant. These policies in recent weeks have received the approval of the people of the United States, and they have, I am sure, the sympathy of the other Nations here assembled.

There are many other causes for war among them, long-festering feuds, unsettled frontiers, territorial rivalries. But these sources of danger which still exist in the Americas, I am thankful to say, are not only few in number but already on the way to peaceful adjudication. While the settlement of such controversies may necessarily involve adjustments at home or in our relations with our neighbors which may appear to involve material sacrifice, let no man or woman forget that there is no profit in war. Sacrifices in the cause of peace are infinitesimal compared with the holocaust of war.

Peace comes from the spirit and must be grounded in faith. In seeking peace, perhaps we can best begin by proudly affirming the faith of the Americas: the faith in freedom and its fulfillment, which has proved a mighty fortress beyond reach of successful attack in half the world.

That faith arises from a common hope and a common design given us by our fathers in differing form but with a single aim: freedom and security of the individual, which has become the foundation of our peace.

If, then, by making war in our midst impossible, and if within ourselves and among ourselves we can give greater freedom and fulfillment to the individual lives of our citizens, the democratic form of representative government will have justified the high hopes of the liberating fathers. Democracy is still the hope of the world. If we in our generation can continue its successful application in the Americas, it will spread and supersede other methods by which men are governed and which seem to most of us to run counter to our ideals of human liberty and human progress.

Three centuries of history sowed the seeds which grew into our Nations; the fourth century saw those Nations become equal and free and brought us to a common system of constitutional government; the fifth century is giving to us a common meeting ground of mutual help and understanding. Our Hemisphere has at last come of age. We are here assembled to show its unity to the world. We took from our ancestors a great dream. We here offer it back as a great unified reality.

Finally, in expressing our faith of the Western World, let us affirm:

That we maintain and defend the democratic form of constitutional representative government.

That through such government we can more greatly provide a wider distribution of culture, of education, of thought, and of free expression.

That through it we can obtain a greater security of life for our citizens and a more equal opportunity for them to prosper.

That through it we can best foster commerce and the exchange of art and science between Nations.

That through it we can avoid the rivalry of armaments, avert hatreds, and encourage good-will and true justice.

That through it we offer hope for peace and a more abundant life to the peoples of the whole world.

But this faith of the Western World will not be complete if we fail to affirm our faith in God. In the whole history of mankind, far back into the dim past before man knew how to record thoughts or events, the human race has been distinguished from other forms of life by the existence, the fact, of religion. Periodic attempts to deny God have always come and will always come to naught.

In the constitution and in the practice of our Nations is the right of freedom of religion. But this ideal, these words, presuppose a belief and a trust in God.

The faith of the Americas, therefore, lies in the spirit. The systems, the sisterhood, of the Americas is impregnable so long as her Nations maintain that spirit.

In that faith and spirit we will have peace over the Western World. In that faith and spirit we will all watch and guard our Hemisphere. In that faith and spirit may we also, with God's help, offer hope to our brethren overseas.

Second Inaugural Address

"Whether we provide enough for those who have too little"

(January 20, 1937)

When four years ago we met to inaugurate President, the Republic, single-minded in anxiety, stood in spirit here. We dedicated ourselves to the fulfillment of a vision — to speed the time when there would be for all the people that security and peace essential to the pursuit of happiness. We of the Republic pledged ourselves to drive from the temple of our ancient faith those who had profaned it; to end by action, tireless and unafraid, the stagnation and despair of that day. We did those first things first.

Our covenant with ourselves did not stop there. Instinctively we recognized a deeper need — the need to find through government the instrument of our united purpose to solve for the individual the ever-rising problems of a complex civilization. Repeated attempts at their solution without the aid of government had left us baffled and bewildered. For, without that aid, we had been unable to create those moral controls over the services of science which are necessary to make science a useful servant instead of a ruthless master of mankind. To do this we knew that we must find practical controls over blind economic forces and blindly selfish men.

We of the Republic sensed the truth that democratic government has innate capacity to protect its people against disasters once considered inevitable, to solve problems once considered unsolvable. We would not admit that we could not find a way to master economic epidemics just as, after centuries of fatalistic suffering, we had found a way to master epidemics of disease. We refused to leave the problems of our common welfare to be solved by the winds of chance and the hurricanes of disaster.

In this we Americans were discovering no wholly new truth; we were writing a new chapter in our book of self-government.

This year marks the one hundred and fiftieth anniversary of the Constitutional Convention which made us a nation. At that Convention our forefathers found the way out of the chaos which followed the Revolutionary War; they created a strong government with powers of united action sufficient then and now to solve problems utterly beyond individual or local solution. A century and a half ago they established the Federal Government in order to promote the general welfare and secure the blessings of liberty to the American people.

Today we invoke those same powers of government to achieve the same objectives.

Four years of new experience have not belied our historic instinct. They hold out the clear hope that government within communities, government within the separate States, and government of the United States can do the things the times require, without yielding its democracy. Our tasks in the last four years did not force democracy to take a holiday.

Nearly all of us recognize that as intricacies of human relationships increase, so power to govern them also must increase power to stop evil; power to do good. The essential democracy of our Nation and the safety of our people depend not upon the absence of power, but upon lodging it with those whom the people can change or continue at stated intervals through an honest and free system of elections. The Constitution of 1787 did not make our democracy impotent.

In fact, in these last four years, we have made the exercise of all power more democratic; for we have begun to bring private autocratic powers into their proper subordination to the public's government. The legend that they were invincible above and beyond the processes of a democracy has been shattered. They have been challenged and beaten.

Our progress out of the depression is obvious. But that is not all that you and I mean by the new order of things. Our pledge was not merely to do a patchwork job with second-hand materials. By using the new materials of social justice we have undertaken to erect on the old foundations a more enduring structure for the better use of future generations.

In that purpose we have been helped by achievements of mind and spirit. Old truths have been relearned; untruths have been unlearned. We have always known that heedless self-interest was bad morals; we know now that it is bad economics. Out of the collapse of a prosperity whose builders boasted their practicality has come the conviction that in the long run economic morality pays. We are beginning to wipe out the line that divides the practical from the ideal; and in so doing we are fashioning an instrument of unimagined power for the establishment of a morally better world.

This new understanding undermines the old admiration of worldly success as such. We are beginning to abandon our tolerance of the abuse of power by those who betray for profit the elementary decencies of life.

In this process evil things formerly accepted will not be so easily condoned. Hard-headedness will not so easily excuse hardheartedness. We are moving toward an era of good feeling.

But we realize that there can be no era of good feeling save among men of good will.

For these reasons I am justified in believing that the greatest change we have witnessed has been the change in the moral climate of America.

Among men of good will, science and democracy together offer an ever-richer life and ever-larger satisfaction to the individual. With this change in our moral climate and our rediscovered ability to improve our economic order, we have set our feet upon the road of enduring progress.

Shall we pause now and turn our back upon the road that lies ahead? Shall we call this the promised land? Or, shall we continue on our way? For "each age is a dream that is dying, or one that is coming to birth."

Many voices are heard as we face a great decision. Comfort says, "Tarry a while." Opportunism says, "This is a good spot." Timidity asks, "How difficult is the road ahead?"

True, we have come far from the days of stagnation and despair. Vitality has been preserved. Courage and confidence have been restored. Mental and moral horizons have been extended.

But our present gains were won under the pressure of more than ordinary circumstance. Advance became imperative under the goad of fear and suffering. The times were on the side of progress.

To hold to progress today, however, is more difficult. Dulled conscience, irresponsibility, and ruthless self-interest already reappear. Such symptoms of prosperity may become portents of disaster! Prosperity already tests the persistence of our progressive purpose.

Let us ask again: Have we reached the goal of our vision of that fourth day of March, 1933? Have we found our happy valley?

I see a great nation, upon a great continent, blessed with a great wealth of natural resources. Its hundred and thirty million people are at peace among themselves; they are making their country a good neighbor among the nations. I see a United States which can demonstrate that, under democratic methods of government, national wealth can be translated into a spreading volume of human comforts hitherto unknown, and the lowest standard of living can be raised far above the level of mere subsistence.

But here is the challenge to our democracy: In this nation I see tens of millions of its citizens — a substantial part of its whole population — who at this very moment are denied the greater part of what the very lowest standards of today call the necessities of life.

I see millions of families trying to live on incomes so meager that the pall of family disaster hangs over them day by day.

I see millions whose daily lives in city and on farm continue under conditions labeled indecent by a so-called polite society half a century ago.

I see millions denied education, recreation, and the opportunity to better their lot and the lot of their children.

I see millions lacking the means to buy the products of farm and factory and by their poverty denying work and productiveness to many other millions.

I see one-third of a nation ill-housed, ill-clad, ill-nourished.

It is not in despair that I paint you that picture. I paint it for you in hope — because the Nation, seeing and understanding the injustice in it, proposes to paint it out. We are determined to make every American citizen the subject of his country's interest and concern; and we will never regard any faithful, law-abiding group within our borders as superfluous. The test of our progress is not whether we add more to the abundance of those who have much; it is whether we provide enough for those who have too little.

If I know aught of the spirit and purpose of our Nation, we will not listen to Comfort, Opportunism, and Timidity. We will carry on.

Overwhelmingly, we of the Republic are men and women of good will; men and women who have more than warm hearts of dedication; men and women who have cool heads and willing hands of practical purpose as well. They will insist that every agency of popular government use effective instruments to carry out their will.

Government is competent when all who compose it work as trustees for the whole people. It can make constant progress when it keeps abreast of all the facts. It can obtain justified support and legitimate criticism when the people receive true information of all that government does.

If I know aught of the will of our people, they will demand that these conditions of effective government shall be created and maintained. They will demand a nation uncorrupted by cancers of injustice and, therefore, strong among the nations in its example of the will to peace.

Today we reconsecrate our country to long-cherished ideals in a suddenly changed civilization. In every land there are always at work forces that drive men apart and forces that draw men together. In our personal ambitions we are individualists. But in our seeking for economic and political progress as a nation, we all go up, or else we all go down, as one people.

To maintain a democracy of effort requires a vast amount of patience in dealing with differing methods, a vast amount of humility. But out of the confusion of many voices rises an understanding of dominant public need. Then political leadership can voice common ideals, and aid in their realization.

In taking again the oath of office as President of the United States, I assume the solemn obligation of leading the American people forward along the road over which they have chosen to advance.

While this duty rests upon me I shall do my utmost to speak their purpose and to do their will, seeking Divine guidance to help us each and every one to give light to them that sit in darkness and to guide our feet into the way of peace.

Address at Chicago

The "Quarantine" Speech

(October 5, 1937)

I am glad to come once again to Chicago and especially to have the opportunity of taking part in the dedication of this important project of civic betterment.

On my trip across the continent and back I have been shown many evidences of the result of common sense cooperation between municipalities and the Federal Government, and I have been greeted by tens of thousands of Americans who have told me in every look and word that their material and spiritual well-being has made great strides forward in the past few years.

And yet, as I have seen with my own eyes, the prosperous farms, the thriving factories and the busy railroads, as I have seen the happiness and security and peace which covers our wide land, almost inevitably I have been compelled to contrast our peace with very different scenes being enacted in other parts of the world.

It is because the people of the United States under modern conditions must, for the sake of their own future, give thought to the rest of the world, that I, as the responsible executive head of the Nation, have chosen this great inland city and this gala occasion to speak to you on a subject of definite national importance.

The political situation in the world, which of late has been growing progressively worse, is such as to cause grave concern and anxiety to all the peoples and nations who wish to live in peace and amity with their neighbors.

Some fifteen years ago the hopes of mankind for a continuing era of international peace were raised to great heights when more than sixty nations solemnly pledged themselves not to resort to arms in furtherance of their national aims and policies. The high aspirations expressed in the Briand-Kellogg Peace Pact and the hopes for peace thus raised have of late given way to a haunting fear of calamity. The present reign of terror and international lawlessness began a few years ago.

It began through unjustified interference in the internal affairs of other nations or the invasion of alien territory in violation of treaties; and has now reached a stage where the very foundations of civilization are seriously threatened. The landmarks and traditions which have marked the progress of civilization toward a condition of law, order and justice are being wiped away.

Without a declaration of war and without warning or justification of any kind, civilians, including vast numbers of women and children, are being ruthlessly murdered with bombs from the air. In times of so-called peace, ships are being attacked and sunk by submarines without cause or notice. Nations are fomenting and taking sides in civil warfare in nations that have never done them any harm. Nations claiming freedom for themselves deny it to others.

Innocent peoples, innocent nations, are being cruelly sacrificed to a greed for power and supremacy which is devoid of all sense of justice and humane considerations.

To paraphrase a recent author "perhaps we foresee a time when men, exultant in the technique of homicide, will rage so hotly over the world that every precious thing will be in danger, every book and picture and harmony, every treasure garnered through two millenniums, the small, the delicate, the defenseless—all will be lost or wrecked or utterly destroyed."

If those things come to pass in other parts of the world, let no one imagine that America will escape, that America may expect mercy, that this Western Hemisphere will not be attacked and that it will continue tranquilly and peacefully to carry on the ethics and the arts of civilization.

If those days come "there will be no safety by arms, no help from authority, no answer in science. The storm will rage till every flower of culture is trampled and all human beings are leveled in a vast chaos."

If those days are not to come to pass—if we are to have a world in which we can breathe freely and live in amity without fear—the peace-loving nations must make a concerted effort to uphold laws and principles on which alone peace can rest secure.

The peace-loving nations must make a concerted effort in opposition to those violations of treaties and those ignorings of humane instincts which today are creating a state of international anarchy and instability from which there is no escape through mere isolation or neutrality.

Those who cherish their freedom and recognize and respect the equal right of their neighbors to be free and live in peace, must work together for the triumph of law and moral principles in order that peace, justice and confidence may prevail in the world. There must be a return to a belief in the pledged word, in the value of a signed treaty. There must be recognition of the fact that national morality is as vital as private morality.

A bishop wrote me the other day: "It seems to me that something greatly needs to be said in behalf of ordinary humanity against the present practice of carrying the horrors of war to helpless civilians, especially women and children. It may be that such a protest might be regarded by many, who claim to be realists, as futile, but may it not be that the heart of mankind is so filled with horror at the present needless suffering that that force could be mobilized in sufficient volume to lessen such cruelty in the days ahead. Even though it may take twenty years, which God forbid, for civilization to make effective its corporate protest against this barbarism, surely strong voices may hasten the day."

There is a solidarity and interdependence about the modern world, both technically and morally, which makes it impossible for any nation completely to isolate itself from economic and political upheavals in the rest of the world, especially when such upheavals appear to be spreading and not declining. There can be no stability or peace either within nations or between nations except under laws and moral standards adhered to by all International anarchy destroys every foundation for peace. It jeopardizes either the immediate or the future security of every nation, large or small. It is, therefore, a matter of vital interest and concern to the people of the United States that the sanctity of international treaties and the maintenance of international morality be restored.

The overwhelming majority of the peoples and nations of the world today want to live in peace. They seek the removal of barriers against trade. They want to exert themselves in industry, in agriculture and in business, that they may increase their wealth through the production of wealth-producing goods rather than striving to produce military planes and bombs and machine guns and cannon for the destruction of human lives and useful property.

In those nations of the world which seem to be piling armament on armament for purposes of aggression, and those other nations which fear acts of aggression against them and their security, a very high proportion of their national income is being spent directly for armaments. It runs from thirty to as high as fifty percent. We are fortunate. The proportion that we in the United States spend is far less — eleven or twelve percent.

How happy we are that the circumstances of the moment permit us to put our money into bridges and boulevards, dams and reforestation, the conservation of our soil and many other kinds of useful works rather than into huge standing armies and vast supplies of implements of war.

I am compelled and you are compelled, nevertheless, to look ahead. The peace, the freedom and the security of ninety percent of the population of the world is being jeopardized by the remaining ten percent. who are threatening a breakdown of all international order and law. Surely the ninety percent who want to live in peace under law and in accordance with moral standards that have received almost universal acceptance through the centuries, can and must find some way to make their will prevail.

The situation is definitely of universal concern. The questions involved relate not merely to violations of specific provisions of particular treaties; they are questions of war and of peace, of international law and especially of principles of humanity. It is true that they involve definite violations of agreements, and especially of the Covenant of the League of Nations, the Briand-Kellogg Pact and the Nine Power Treaty. But they also involve problems of world economy, world security and world humanity.

It is true that the moral consciousness of the world must recognize the importance of removing injustices and well-founded grievances; but at the same time it must be aroused to the cardinal necessity of honoring sanctity of treaties, of respecting the rights and liberties of others and of putting an end to acts of international aggression.

It seems to be unfortunately true that the epidemic of world lawlessness is spreading.

When an epidemic of physical disease starts to spread, the community approves and joins in a quarantine of the patients in order to protect the health of the community against the spread of the disease.

It is my determination to pursue a policy of peace. It is my determination to adopt every practicable measure to avoid involvement in war. It ought to be inconceivable that in this modern era, and in the face of experience, any nation could be so foolish and ruthless as to run the risk of plunging the whole world into war by invading and violating, in contravention of solemn treaties, the territory of other nations that have done them no real harm and are too weak to protect themselves adequately. Yet the peace of the world and the welfare and security of every nation, including our own, is today being threatened by that very thing.

No nation which refuses to exercise forbearance and to respect the freedom and rights of others can long remain strong and retain the confidence and respect of other nations. No nation ever loses its dignity or its good standing by conciliating its differences, and by exercising great patience with, and consideration for, the rights of other nations.

War is a contagion, whether it be declared or undeclared. It can engulf states and peoples remote from the original scene of hostilities. We are determined to keep out of war, yet we cannot insure ourselves against the disastrous effects of war and the dangers of involvement. We are adopting such measures as will minimize our risk of involvement, but we cannot have complete protection in a world of disorder in which confidence and security have broken down.

If civilization is to survive the principles of the Prince of Peace must be restored. Trust between nations must be revived.

Most important of all, the will for peace on the part of peace-loving nations must express itself to the end that nations that may be tempted to violate their agreements and the rights of others will desist from such a course. There must be positive endeavors to preserve peace.

America hates war. America hopes for peace. Therefore, America actively engages in the search for peace.

Message To The Congress Recommending Increased Armament For National Defense

"Every effort at peace, but protect our nation".

(January 28, 1938)

To the Congress:

The Congress knows that for many years this Government has sought in many Capitals with the leaders of many Governments to find a way to limit and reduce armaments and to establish at least the probability of world peace.

The Congress is aware also that while these efforts, supported by the hopes of the American people, continue and will continue they have nevertheless failed up to the present time.

We, as a peaceful Nation, cannot and will not abandon active search for an agreement among the nations to limit armaments and end aggression. But it is clear that until such agreement is reached — and I have not given up hope of it — we are compelled to think of our own national safety.

It is with the deepest regret that I report to you that armaments increase today at an unprecedented and alarming rate. It is an ominous fact that at least one-fourth of the world's population is involved in merciless devastating conflict in spite of the fact that most people in most countries, including those where conflict rages, wish to live at peace. Armies are fighting in the Far East and in Europe; thousands of civilians are being driven from their homes and bombed from the air. Tension throughout the world is high.

As Commander-in-Chief of the Army and Navy of the United States it is my constitutional duty to report to the Congress that our national defense is, in the light of the increasing armaments of other Nations, inadequate for purposes of national security and requires increase for that reason.

In spite of the well-known fact that the American standard of living makes our ships, our guns and our planes cost more for construction than in any other Nation and that the maintenance of them and of our Army and Navy personnel is more expensive than in any other Nation, it is also true that the proportion of the cost of our military and naval forces to the total income of our citizens or to the total cost of our Government is far lower than in the case of any other great Nation.

Specifically and solely because of the piling up of additional land and sea armaments in other countries, in such manner as to involve a threat to world peace and security, I make the following recommendations to the Congress:

(1) That there be authorized for the Army of the United States additions to anti-aircraft materiel in the sum of $8,800,000 and that of this sum $6,800,000 be appropriated for the fiscal year 1939.

(2) That there be authorized and appropriated for the better establishment of an Enlisted Reserve for the Army the sum of 8450,000.

(3) That there be authorized the expenditure of $6,080,000 for the manufacture of gauges, dies and other aids to manufacture of Army materiel, the sum of $5,000,000 thereof to be expended during the fiscal year 1939.

(4) That the sum of $2,000,000 be authorized and appropriated toward the making up of deficiencies in ammunition for the Army.

(5) That the existing authorized building program for increases and replacements in the Navy be increased by 20 per cent.

(6) That this Congress authorize and appropriate for the laying down of two additional battleships and two additional cruisers during the calendar year 1938. This will call for the expenditure of a very small amount of Government funds during the fiscal year 1939.

(7) That the Congress authorize and appropriate a sum not to exceed $15,000,000 for the construction of a number of new types of small vessels, such construction to be regarded as experimental in the light of new developments among Navies; and to include the preparation of plans for other types of ships in event that it may be necessary to construct such ships in the future.

I believe also that the time has come for the Congress to enact legislation aimed at the prevention of profiteering in time of war and the equalization of the burdens of possible war. Such legislation has been the subject for many years of full study in this and previous Congresses.

It is necessary for all of us to realize that the unfortunate world conditions of today have resulted too often in the discarding of those principles and treaties which underlie international law and order; and in the entrance of many new factors into the actual conduct of war.

Adequate defense means that for the protection not only of our coasts but also of our communities far removed from the coast, we must keep any potential enemy many hundred miles away from our continental limits.

We cannot assume that our defense would be limited to one ocean and one coast and that the other ocean and the other coast would with certainty be safe. We cannot be certain that the connecting link, the Panama Canal, would be safe. Adequate defense affects therefore the simultaneous defense of every part of the United States of America.

It is our clear duty to further every effort toward peace but at the same time to protect our Nation. That is the purpose of these recommendations. Such protection is and will be based not on aggression but on defense.

Dedication of a Memorial to the Northwest Territory

"The government is ourselves and not an alien power over us".

(July 8, 1938)

Governor Davey, Senator Bulkley, Chairman White and You the People of the Northwest Territory:

Long before 1788 there were white men here, "spying out this land of Canaan." An intrepid outpost breed they were—the scouts and the skirmishers of the great American migration. The sight of smoke from neighbors' chimneys might have worried them. But Indians and redcoats did not.

Long before 1788, at Kaskaskia and Vincennes, with scant help from the Seaboard, they had held their beloved wilderness for themselves—and for us—with their own bare hands and their own long rifles. But their symbol is Vincennes, not Marietta.

Here, with all honor to the scouts and the skirmishers, we celebrate the coming of a different type of men and women — the first battalions of that organized army of occupation which transplanted from over the Alleghenies whole little civilizations that took root and grew. They were giving expression to a genius for organized colonization, carefully planned and ordered under law.

The men who came here before 1788 came as Leif Ericson's men to Vineland, in a spirit all of adventure. But the men and women of the Ohio Company who came to Marietta came rather like the men and women of the Massachusetts Bay Company to Boston, an organized society, unafraid to meet temporary adventure, but serious in seeking permanent security for men and women and children and homes. Many of them were destined to push on; but most came intending to stay. Such people may not be the first to conquer the earth, but they will always be the last to possess it.

Right behind the men and women who established Marietta one hundred and fifty years ago moved that instrument of law and order and cooperation — government. A representative of the national government entered Marietta to administer the Northwest Territory under the famous Northwest Ordinance. And what we are celebrating today is this establishment of the first civil government west of the original thirteen states.

Three provisions of the Northwest Ordinance I always like to remember.

It provided that "no person demeaning himself in a peaceable and orderly manner shall ever be molested on account of his mode of worship or for religious sentiment in the said territory."

It provided that "religion, morality and knowledge being necessary to good government and the happiness of mankind, schools and means of education shall forever be encouraged."

And it provided for the perpetual prohibition of slavery in the Territory.

Free, educated, God-fearing men and women—that is what the thirteen states hoped the new West would exemplify. It has well fulfilled that hope.

Every generation meets substantially the same problems under its own different set of circumstances. Anyone speculating on our great migration westward is struck with the human parallel between the driving force behind that migration and the driving force behind the great social exploration we are carrying on today.

Most of the people who went out to Ohio in 1788 and who followed wave on wave for another hundred years went to improve their economic lot. In other words, they were following the same yearning for security which is driving us forward today.

At the end of the wagon ruts there was something worth the physical risks. The standard of life in a log cabin amid fields still blackened with half-burned stumps was not high, but it was certain. A family, or at most a township, could be a whole self-sufficing economic system—plenty of food to eat if a man would but reach out and shoot or cultivate it; plenty of warm clothes if the women of the family were willing to spin; always a tight roof over the family's head if the little community would respond to the call for a roof-raising.

Whatever he used was a man's own; he had the solid joy of possession—of owning his home and his means of livelihood. And if things did not pan out there was always an infinite self-sufficiency beckoning further westward—to new land, new game, new opportunity.

Under such conditions there was so much to get done which men could not get done alone, that the frontiersmen naturally reached out to government as their greatest single instrument of cooperative self-help with the aid of which they could get things done. To them the use of government was but another form of the cooperation of good neighbors.

Government was an indispensable instrument of their daily lives, of the security of their women and their children and their homes and their opportunities. They looked on government not as a thing apart—as a power over our people. They regarded it as a power of the people, as a democratic expression of organized self-help like a frontier husking bee.

There were worried legalists back in the seaboard towns who were sure it was unconstitutional for the Federal Government to help to put roads and railroads and canals through these new territories—who were sure that the nation would never get back the money it was plowing into development of the natural and human resources of the Northwest.

But Abraham Lincoln, who incarnated the spirit of the people who were actually living in the Northwest Territory, summed up their attitude when he said: "The legitimate object of government is to do for a community of people whatever they need to have done, but cannot do at all, or cannot do so well, for themselves, in their separate and individual capacities."

Today, under new conditions, a whole nation, the critical thirteen states and all the West and South that has grown out of them, is on a mental migration, dissatisfied with old conditions, seeking like the little band that came to Marietta to create new conditions of security. And again the people see an ally in their own government.

Many a man does not own his cabin any more; his possessions are a bank deposit.

Scarcely any man can call his neighbors to raise his roof any more—he pays a contractor cash and has to have mortgage financing to find the cash. And if that financing is of the wrong kind or goes bad, he may need help to save his home from foreclosure.

Once old age was safe because there was always something useful which men and women, no matter how old, could do to earn an honorable maintenance. That time is gone; and some new kind of organized old-age insurance has to be provided.

In these perplexities the individual turns, as he has always turned, to the collective security of the willingness of his fellows to cooperate through the use of government to help him and each other. The spirit of the frontier husking bee is found today in carefully-drafted statutes—statutes insuring bank deposits; statutes providing mortgage money for homes through F.H.A.; statutes providing help through H.O.L.C. for those in danger of foreclosure. The cavalry captain who protected the log cabins of the Northwest is now supplanted by legislators, like Senator Bulkley, toiling over the drafting of such statutes and over the efficiency of government machinery to administer them so that such protection and help of government can be extended to the full.

On a thousand fronts, government—state and municipal as well as federal—is playing the same role of the insurer of security for the average man, woman and child that the Army detachments played in the early days of the old Northwest Territory. When you think it through, at the bottom most of the great protective statutes of today are in essence mutual insurance companies, and our recent legislation is not a departure from but a return to the healthy practices of mutual self-help of the early settlers of the Northwest.

Let us not be afraid to help each other—let us never forget that government is ourselves and not an alien power over us. The ultimate rulers of our democracy are not a President and Senators and Congressmen and Government officials but the voters of this country.

I believe that the American people, not afraid of their own capacity to choose forward-looking representatives to run their government, want the same cooperative security and have the same courage to achieve it, in 1938, as in 1788. I am sure they know that we shall always have a frontier—of social and economic problems—and that we must always move in to bring law and order to it. In that confidence I am pushing on. I am sure that the people of the Nation will push on with me.

Address to the Governing Board of the Pan American Union

"The Community of Nations"

(April 14, 1939)

Gentlemen of the Pan American Union:

I am glad to come here today on our Pan American forty-ninth birthday.

The American family of Nations pays honor today to the oldest and most successful association of sovereign Governments which exists in all the world.

Few of us realize that the Pan American organization as we know it, has now attained a longer history and a greater catalogue of achievements than any similar group known to modern history. Justly we can be proud of it. With even more right we can look to it as a symbol of great hope at a time when much of the world finds hope dim and difficult. Never was it more fitting to salute Pan American Day than in the stormy present.

For upwards of half a century the Republics of the Western World have been working together to promote their common civilization under a system of peace. That venture, launched so hopefully fifty years ago, has succeeded. The American family is today a great cooperative group facing a troubled world in serenity and calm.

This success of the Western Hemisphere is sometimes attributed to good fortune. I do not share that view. There are not wanting here all of the usual rivalries, all of the normal human desires for power and expansion, all of the commercial problems. The Americas are sufficiently rich to have been themselves the object of desire on the part of overseas Governments; our traditions in history are as deeply rooted in the Old World as are those of Europe.

It was not accident that prevented South America, and our own West, from sharing the fate of other great areas of the world in the nineteenth century. We have here diversities of race, of language, of custom, of natural resources; and of intellectual forces at least as great as those which prevailed in Europe.

What was it that has protected us from the tragic involvements which are today making the Old World a new cockpit of old struggles? The answer is easily found. A new, and powerful ideal—that of the community of nations—sprang up at the same time that the Americas became free and independent. It was nurtured by statesmen, thinkers and plain people for decades. Gradually it brought together the Pan American group of Governments; today it has fused the thinking of the peoples, and the desires of their responsible representatives toward a common objective.

The result of this thinking through all these years has been to shape a typically American institution. This is the Pan American group, which works in open conference, by open agreement. We hold our conferences not as a result of wars, but as the result of our will to peace.

Elsewhere in the world, to hold conferences such as ours, which meet every five years, it is necessary to fight a major war, until exhaustion or defeat at length brings Governments together to reconstruct their shattered fabrics.

Greeting a conference at Buenos Aires in 1936, I took occasion to say this:

"The madness of a great war in another part of the world would affect us and threaten our good in a hundred ways. And the economic collapse of any Nation or nations must of necessity harm our own prosperity. Can we, the Republics of the New World, help the Old World to avert the catastrophe which impends? Yes, I am confident that we can."

I still have that confidence. There is no fatality which forces the Old World towards new catastrophe. Men are not prisoners of fate, but only prisoners of their own minds. They have within themselves the power to become free at any moment.

Only a few days ago the head of a great Nation referred to his country as a "prisoner" in the Mediterranean. A little later, another chief of state, on learning that a neighbor country had agreed to defend the independence of another neighbor, characterized that agreement as a "threat" and an "encirclement." Yet there is no such thing as encircling or threatening, or imprisoning any peaceful Nation by other peaceful nations. We have reason to know that in our own experience.

For instance, on the occasion of a visit to the neighboring Dominion of Canada last summer, I stated that the United States would join in defending Canada were she ever attacked from overseas. Again at Lima in December last, the twenty-one American Nations joined in a declaration that they would coordinate their common efforts to defend the integrity of their institutions from any attack, direct or indirect.

At Buenos Aires, in 1936, all of us agreed that in the event of any war or threat of war on this continent, we would consult together to remove or obviate that threat. Yet in no case did any

American Nation regard any of these understandings as making any one of them a "prisoner," or as "encircling" any American country, or as a threat of any sort or kind.

Measures of this kind taken in this hemisphere are taken as guarantees, not of war but of peace, for the simple reason that no Nation on this hemisphere has any will to aggression, or any desire to establish dominance or mastery. Equally, because we are interdependent, and because we know it, no American Nation seeks to deny any neighbor access to the economic and other resources which it must have to live in prosperity.

In these circumstances, my friends, dreams of conquest appear to us as ridiculous as they are criminal. Pledges designed to prevent aggression, accompanied by the open doors of trade and intercourse, and bound together by common will to cooperate peacefully, make warfare between us as outworn and useless as the weapons of the Stone-Age. We may proudly boast that we have begun to realize in Pan American relations what civilization in intercourse between countries really means.

If that process can be successful here, is it too much to hope that a similar intellectual and spiritual process may succeed elsewhere? Do we really have to assume that nations can find no better methods of realizing their destinies than those which were used by the Huns and the Vandals fifteen hundred years ago?

The American peace which we celebrate today has no quality of weakness in it! We are prepared to maintain it, and to defend it to the fullest extent of our strength, matching force to force if any attempt is made to subvert our institutions, or to impair the independence of any one of our group.

Should the method of attack be that of economic pressure, I pledge that my country will also give economic support, so that no American Nation need surrender any fraction of its sovereign freedom to maintain its economic welfare. This is the spirit and intent of the Declaration of Lima: the solidarity of the continent.

The American family of Nations may also rightfully claim, now, to speak to the rest of the world. We have an interest, wider than that of the mere defense of our sea-ringed continent. We know now that the development of the next generation will so narrow the oceans separating us from the Old World, that our customs and our actions are necessarily involved with hers, whether we like it or not.

Beyond question, within a scant few years air fleets will cross the ocean as easily as today they cross the closed European seas. Economic functioning of the world becomes therefore necessarily a unit; no interruption of it anywhere can fail, in the future, to disrupt economic life everywhere.

The past generation in Pan American matters was concerned with constructing the principles and the mechanisms through which this hemisphere would work together. But the next generation will be concerned with the methods by which the New World can live together in peace with the Old.

The issue is really whether our civilization is to be dragged into the tragic vortex of unending militarism punctuated by periodic wars, or whether we shall be able to maintain the ideal of peace, individuality and civilization as the fabric of our lives. We have the right to say that there shall not be an organization of world affairs which permits us no choice but to turn our countries into barracks, unless we are to be the vassals of some conquering empire.

The truest defense of the peace of our hemisphere must always lie in the hope that our sister nations beyond the seas will break the bonds of the ideas that constrain them toward perpetual warfare. By example we can at least show them the possibility. We, too, have a stake in world affairs.

Our will to peace can be as powerful as our will to mutual defense; it can command greater loyalty, greater devotion, greater discipline than that enlisted elsewhere for temporary conquest or equally futile glory. It will have its voice in determining the order of world affairs in the days to come.

This, gentlemen, is the living message which the New World can and does send to the Old. It can be light opening on dark waters. It shows the path of peace.

Address at the University of Virginia

The "Stab in the Back" Speech

(June 10, 1940)

President Newcomb, my friends of the University of Virginia:

I notice by the program that I am asked to address the class of 1940. I avail myself of that privilege. But I also take this very apt occasion to speak to many other classes that have graduated through all the years, classes that are still in the period of study, not alone in the schools of learning of the Nation, but classes that have come up through the great schools of experience; in other words a cross section of the country, just as you who graduate today are a cross section of the Nation as a whole.

Every generation of young men and women in America has questions to ask the world. Most of the time they are the simple but nevertheless difficult questions, questions of work to do, opportunities to find, ambitions to satisfy.

But every now and again in the history of the Republic a different kind of question presents itself — a question that asks, not about the future of an individual or even of a generation, but about the future of the country, the future of the American people.

There was such a time at the beginning of our history as a Nation. Young people asked themselves in those days what lay ahead, not for themselves, but for the new United States.

There was such a time again in the seemingly endless years of the War Between the States. Young men and young women on both sides of the line asked themselves, not what trades or professions they would enter, what lives they would make, but what was to become of the country they had known.

There is such a time again today. Again today the young men and the young women of America ask themselves with earnestness and with deep concern this same question: "What is to become of the country we know?"

Now they ask it with even greater anxiety than before. They ask, not only what the future holds for this Republic, but what the future holds for all peoples and all nations that have been living under democratic forms of Government—under the free institutions of a free people.

It is understandable to all of us that they should ask this question. They read the words of those who are telling them that the ideal of individual liberty, the ideal of free franchise, the ideal of peace through justice, are decadent ideals. They read the word and hear the boast of those who say that a belief in force—force directed by self-chosen leaders—is the new and vigorous system which will overrun the earth. They have seen the ascendancy of this philosophy of force in nation after nation where free institutions and individual liberties were once maintained.

It is natural and understandable that the younger generation should first ask itself what the extension of the philosophy of force to all the world would lead to ultimately. We see today in stark reality some of the consequences of what we call the machine age.

Where control of machines has been retained in the hands of mankind as a whole, untold benefits have accrued to mankind. For mankind was then the master; and the machine was the servant.

But in this new system of force the mastery of the machine is not in the hands of mankind. It is in the control of infinitely small groups of individuals who rule without a single one of the democratic sanctions that we have known. The machine in hands of irresponsible conquerors becomes the master; mankind is not only the servant; it is the victim, too. Such mastery abandons with deliberate contempt all the moral values to which even this young country for more than three hundred years has been accustomed and dedicated.

Surely the new philosophy proves from month to month that it could have no possible conception of the way of life or the way of thought of a nation whose origins go back to Jamestown and Plymouth Rock.

Conversely, neither those who spring from that ancient stock nor those who have come hither in later years can be indifferent to the destruction of freedom in their ancestral lands across the sea.

Perception of danger to our institutions may come slowly or it may come with a rush and a shock as it has to the people of the United States in the past few months. This perception of danger has come to us clearly and overwhelmingly; and we perceive the peril in a world-wide arena—an arena that may become so narrowed that only the Americas will retain the ancient faiths.

Some indeed still hold to the now somewhat obvious delusion that we of the United States can safely permit the United States to become a lone island, a lone island in a world dominated by the philosophy of force.

Such an island may be the dream of those who still talk and vote as isolationists. Such an island represents to me and to the overwhelming majority of Americans today a helpless nightmare of a people without freedom—the nightmare of a people lodged in prison, handcuffed, hungry, and fed through the bars from day to day by the contemptuous, unpitying masters of other continents.

It is natural also that we should ask ourselves how now we can prevent the building of that prison and the placing of ourselves in the midst of it.

Let us not hesitate—all of us—to proclaim certain truths. Overwhelmingly we, as a nation—and this applies to all the other American nations—are convinced that military and naval victory for the gods of force and hate would endanger the institutions of democracy in the western world, and that equally, therefore, the whole of our sympathies lies with those nations that are giving their life blood in combat against these forces.

The people and the Government of the United States have seen with the utmost regret and with grave disquiet the decision of the Italian Government to engage in the hostilities now raging in Europe.

More than three months ago the Chief of the Italian Government sent me word that because of the determination of Italy to limit, so far as might be possible, the spread of the European conflict, more than two hundred millions of people in the region of the Mediterranean had been enabled to escape the suffering and the 'devastation of war.

I informed the Chief of the Italian Government that this desire on the part of Italy to prevent the war from spreading met with full sympathy and response on the part of the Government and the people of the United States, and I expressed the earnest hope of this Government and of this people that this policy on the part of Italy might be continued. I made it clear that in the opinion of the Government of the United States any extension of hostilities in the region of the Mediterranean might result in a still greater enlargement of the scene of the conflict, the conflict in the Near East and in Africa and that if this came to pass no one could foretell how much greater the theater of the war eventually might become.

Again on a subsequent occasion, not so long ago, recognizing that certain aspirations of Italy might form the basis of discussions among the powers most specifically concerned, I offered, in a message addressed to the Chief of the Italian Government, to send to the Governments of France and of Great Britain such specific indications of the desires of Italy to obtain readjustments with regard to her position as the Chief of the Italian Government might desire to transmit through me. While making it clear that the Government of the United States in such an event could not and would not assume responsibility for the nature of the proposals submitted nor for agreements which might thereafter be reached, I proposed that if Italy would refrain from entering the war I would be willing to ask assurances from the other powers concerned that they would faithfully execute any agreement so reached and that Italy's voice in any future peace conference would have the same authority as if Italy had actually taken part in the war, as a belligerent.

Unfortunately to the regret of all of us and the regret of humanity, the Chief of the Italian Government was unwilling to accept the procedure suggested and he has made no counter proposal.

This Government directed its efforts to doing what it could to work for the preservation of peace in the Mediterranean area, and it likewise expressed its willingness to endeavor to cooperate with the Government of Italy when the appropriate occasion arose for the creation of a more stable world order, through the reduction of armaments, and through the construction of a more liberal international economic system which would assure to all powers equality of opportunity in the world's markets and in the securing of raw materials on equal terms.

I have likewise, of course, felt it necessary in my communications to Signor Mussolini to express the concern of the Government of the United States because of the fact that any extension of the war in the region of the Mediterranean would inevitably result in great prejudice to the ways of life and Government and to the trade and commerce of all the American Republics.

The Government of Italy has now chosen to preserve what it terms its "freedom of action" and to fulfill what it states are its promises to Germany. In so doing it has manifested disregard for the rights and security of other nations, disregard for the lives of the peoples of those nations which are directly threatened by this spread of the war; and has evidenced its unwillingness to find the means through pacific negotiations for the satisfaction of what it believes are its legitimate aspirations.

On this tenth day of June, 1940, the hand that held the dagger has struck it into the back of its neighbor.

On this tenth day of June, 1940, in this University founded by the first great American teacher of democracy, we send forth our prayers and our hopes to those beyond the seas who are maintaining with magnificent valor their battle for freedom.

In our American unity, we will pursue two obvious and simultaneous courses; we will extend to the opponents of force the material resources of this nation; and, at the same time, we will harness and speed up the use of those resources in order that we ourselves in the Americas may have equipment and training equal to the task of any emergency and every defense.

All roads leading to the accomplishment of these objectives must be kept clear of obstructions. We will not slow down or detour. Signs and signals call for speed — full speed ahead.

It is right that each new generation should ask questions. But in recent months the principal question has been somewhat simplified. Once more the future of the nation and of the American people is at stake.

We need not and we will not, in any way, abandon our continuing effort to make democracy work within our borders. We still insist on the need for vast improvements in our own social and economic life. But that is a component part of national defense itself.

The program unfolds swiftly and into that program will fit the responsibility and the opportunity of every man and woman in the land to preserve his and her heritage in days of peril.

I call for effort, courage, sacrifice, devotion. Granting the love of freedom, all of these are possible.

And the love of freedom is still fierce and steady in the nation today.

Acceptance Speech at the Democratic National Convention

"It is not an ordinary war".

(July 19, 1940)

Members of the Convention — my friends:

It is very late; but I have felt that you would rather that I speak to you now than wait until tomorrow.

It is with a very full heart that I speak tonight. I must confess that I do so with mixed feelings — because I find myself, as almost everyone does sooner or later in his lifetime, in a conflict between deep personal desire for retirement on the one hand, and that quiet, invisible thing called "conscience" on the other.

Because there are self-appointed commentators and interpreters who will seek to misinterpret or question motives, I speak in a somewhat personal vein; and I must trust to the good faith and common sense of the American people to accept my own good faith and to do their own interpreting.

When, in 1936, I was chosen by the voters for a second time as President, it was my firm intention to turn over the responsibilities of Government to other hands at the end of my term. That conviction remained with me. Eight years in the Presidency, following a period of bleak depression, and covering one world crisis after another, would normally entitle any man to the relaxation that comes from honorable retirement.

During the spring of 1939, world events made it clear to all but the blind or the partisan that a great war in Europe had become not merely a possibility but a probability, and that such a war would of necessity deeply affect the future of this nation.

When the conflict first broke out last September, it was still my intention to announce clearly and simply, at an early date, that under no conditions would I accept reelection. This fact was well known to my friends, and I think was understood by many citizens.

It soon became evident, however, that such a public statement on my part would be unwise from the point of view of sheer public duty. As President of the United States, it was my clear duty, with the aid of the Congress, to preserve our neutrality, to shape our program of defense, to meet rapid changes, to keep our domestic affairs adjusted to shifting world conditions, and to sustain the policy of the Good Neighbor.

It was also my obvious duty to maintain to the utmost the influence of this mighty nation in our effort to prevent the spread of war, and to sustain by all legal means those governments threatened by other governments which had rejected the principles of democracy.

Swiftly moving foreign events made necessary swift action at home and beyond the seas. Plans for national defense had to be expanded and adjusted to meet new forms of warfare. American citizens and their welfare had to be safeguarded in many foreign zones of danger. National unity in the United

States became a crying essential in the face of the development of unbelievable types of espionage and international treachery.

Every day that passed called for the postponement of personal plans and partisan debate until the latest possible moment. The normal conditions under which I would have made public declaration of my personal desires were wholly gone.

And so, thinking solely of the national good and of the international scene, I came to the reluctant conclusion that such declaration should not be made before the national Convention. It was accordingly made to you within an hour after the permanent organization of this Convention.

Like any other man, I am complimented by the honor you have done me. But I know you will understand the spirit in which I say that no call of Party alone would prevail upon me to accept reelection to the Presidency.

The real decision to be made in these circumstances is not the acceptance of a nomination, but rather an ultimate willingness to serve if chosen by the electorate of the United States. Many considerations enter into this decision.

During the past few months, with due Congressional approval, we in the United States have been taking steps to implement the total defense of America. I cannot forget that in carrying out this program I have drafted into the service of the nation many men and women, taking them away from important private affairs, calling them suddenly from their homes and their businesses. I have asked them to leave their own work, and to contribute their skill and experience to the cause of their nation.

I, as the head of their Government, have asked them to do this. Regardless of party, regardless of personal convenience, they came—they answered the call. Every single one of them, with one exception, has come to the nation's Capital to serve the nation.

These people, who have placed patriotism above all else, represent those who have made their way to what might be called the top of their professions or industries through their proven skill and experience.

But they alone could not be enough to meet the needs of the times.

Just as a system of national defense based on manpower alone, without the mechanized equipment of modern warfare, is totally insufficient for adequate national defense, so also planes and guns and tanks are wholly insufficient unless they are implemented by the power of men trained to use them.

Such manpower consists not only of pilots and gunners and infantry and those who operate tanks. For every individual in actual combat service, it is necessary for adequate defense that we have ready at hand at least four or five other trained individuals organized for non-combat services.

Because of the millions of citizens involved in the conduct of defense, most right thinking persons are agreed that some form of selection by draft is as necessary and fair today as it was in 1917 and 1918.

Nearly every American is willing to do his share or her share to defend the United States. It is neither just nor efficient to permit that task to fall upon any one section or any one group. For every section and every group depend for their existence upon the survival of the nation as a whole.

Lying awake, as I have, on many nights, I have asked myself whether I have the right, as Commander-in-Chief of the Army and Navy, to call on men and women to serve their country or to train themselves to serve and, at the same time, decline to serve my country in my own personal capacity, if I am called upon to do so by the people of my country.

In times like these—in times of great tension, of great crisis—the compass of the world narrows to a single fact. The fact which dominates our world is the fact of armed aggression, the fact of successful armed aggression, aimed at the form of

Government, the kind of society that we in the United States have chosen and established for ourselves. It is a fact which no one longer doubts, which no one is longer able to ignore.

It is not an ordinary war. It is a revolution imposed by force of arms, which threatens all men everywhere. It is a revolution which proposes not to set men free but to reduce them to slavery—to reduce them to slavery in the interest of a dictatorship which has already shown the nature and the extent of the advantage which it hopes to obtain.

That is the fact which dominates our world and which dominates the lives of all of us, each and every one of us. In the face of the danger which confronts our time, no individual retains or can hope to retain, the right of personal choice which free men enjoy in times of peace. He has a first obligation to serve in the defense of our institutions of freedom—a first obligation to serve his country in whatever capacity his country finds him useful.

Like most men of my age, I had made plans for myself, plans for a private life of my own choice and for my own satisfaction, a life of that kind to begin in January, 1941. These plans, like so many other plans, had been made in a world which now seems as distant as another planet. Today all private plans, all private lives, have been in a sense repealed by an overriding public danger. In the face of that public danger all those who can be of service to the Republic have no choice but to offer themselves for service in those capacities for which they may be fitted.

Those, my friends, are the reasons why I have had to admit to myself, and now to state to you, that my conscience will not let me turn my back upon a call to service.

The right to make that call rests with the people through the American method of a free election. Only the people themselves can draft a President. If such a draft should be made upon me, I say to you, in the utmost simplicity, I will, with God's help, continue to serve with the best of my ability and with the fullness of my strength.

To you, the delegates of this Convention, I express my gratitude for the selection of Henry Wallace for the high office of Vice President of the United States. His first-hand knowledge of the problems of Government in every sphere of life and in every single part of the nation—and indeed of the whole world—qualifies him without reservation. His practical idealism will be of great service to me individually and to the nation as a whole.

And to the Chairman of the National Committee, the Postmaster General of the United States—my old friend Jim Farley—I send, as I have often before and shall many times again, my most affectionate greetings. All of us are sure that he will continue to give all the leadership and support that he possibly can to the cause of American democracy.

In some respects, as I think my good wife suggested an hour or so ago—the next few months will be different from the usual national campaigns of recent years.

Most of you know how important it is that the President of the United States in these days remain close to the seat of Government. Since last Summer I have been compelled to abandon proposed journeys to inspect many of our great national projects from the Alleghenies to the Pacific Coast.

Events move so fast in other parts of the world that it has be come my duty to remain either in the White House itself or at some near-by point where I can reach Washington and even Europe and Asia by direct telephone—where, if need be, I can be back at my desk in the space of a very few hours. And in addition, the splendid work of the new defense machinery will require me to spend vastly more time in conference with the responsible administration heads under me. Finally, the added task which the present crisis has imposed also upon the Congress, compelling them to forego their usual adjournment, calls for constant cooperation between the Executive and

Legislative branches, to the efficiency of which I am glad indeed now to pay tribute.

I do expect, of course, during the coming months to make my usual periodic reports to the country through the medium of press conferences and radio talks. I shall not have the time or the inclination to engage in purely political debate. But I shall never be loath to call the attention of the nation to deliberate or unwitting falsifications of fact, which are sometimes made by political candidates.

I have spoken to you in a very informal and personal way. The exigencies of the day require, however, that I also talk with you about things which transcend any personality and go very deeply to the roots of American civilization.

Our lives have been based on those fundamental freedoms and liberties which we Americans have cherished for a century and a half. The establishment of them and the preservation of them in each succeeding generation have been accomplished through the processes of free elective Government — the democratic-republican form, based on the representative system and the coordination of the executive, the legislative and the judicial branches.

The task of safeguarding our institutions seems to me to be twofold. One must be accomplished, if it becomes necessary, by the armed defense forces of the nation. The other, by the united effort of the men and women of the country to make our Federal and State and local Governments responsive to the growing requirements of modern democracy.

There have been occasions, as we remember, when reactions in the march of democracy have set in, and forward-looking progress has seemed to stop.

But such periods have been followed by liberal and progressive times which have enabled the nation to catch up with new developments in fulfilling new human needs. Such a time has been the past seven years. Because we had seemed to lag in previous years, we have had to develop, speedily and efficiently, the answers to aspirations which had come from every State and every family in the land.

We have sometimes called it social legislation; we have sometimes called it legislation to end the abuses of the past; we have sometimes called it legislation for human security; and we have sometimes called it legislation to better the condition of life of the many millions of our fellow citizens, who could not have the essentials of life or hope for an American standard of living.

Some of us have labeled it a wider and more equitable distribution of wealth in our land. It has included among its aims, to liberalize and broaden the control of vast industries— lodged today in the hands of a relatively small group of individuals of very great financial power.

But all of these definitions and labels are essentially the expression of one consistent thought. They represent a constantly growing sense of human decency, human decency throughout our nation.

This sense of human decency is happily confined to no group or class. You find it in the humblest home. You find it among those who toil, and among the shopkeepers and the farmers of the nation. You find it, to a growing degree, even among those who are listed in that top group which has so much control over the industrial and financial structure of the nation. Therefore, this urge of humanity can by no means be labeled a war of class against class. It is rather a war against poverty and suffering and ill-health and insecurity, a war in which all classes are joining in the interest of a sound and enduring democracy.

I do not believe for a moment, and I know that you do not believe either, that we have fully answered all the needs of human security. But we have covered much of the road. I need not catalogue the milestones of seven years. For every individual and every family in the whole land know that the average of their personal lives has been made safer and sounder and happier than it has ever been before. I do not think they want the gains in these directions to be repealed or even to be placed in the charge of those who would give them mere lip-service with no heart service.

Yes, very much more remains to be done, and I think the voters want the task entrusted to those who believe that the words "human betterment" apply to poor and rich alike.

And I have a sneaking suspicion too, that voters will smile at charges of inefficiency against a Government which has boldly met the enormous problems of banking, and finance and industry which the great efficient bankers and industrialists of the Republican Party left in such hopeless chaos in the famous year 1933.

But we all know that our progress at home and in the other American nations toward this realization of a better human decency — progress along free lines — is gravely endangered by what is happening on other continents. In Europe, many nations, through dictatorships or invasions, have been compelled to abandon normal democratic processes. They have been compelled to adopt forms of government which some call "new and efficient."

They are not new, my friends, they are only a relapse — a relapse into ancient history. The omnipotent rulers of the greater part of modern Europe have guaranteed efficiency, and work, and a type of security.

But the slaves who built the pyramids for the glory of the dictator Pharaohs of Egypt had that kind of security, that kind of efficiency, that kind of corporative state.

So did the inhabitants of that world which extended from Britain to Persia under the undisputed rule of the proconsuls sent out from Rome.

So did the henchmen, the tradesmen, the mercenaries and the slaves of the feudal system which dominated Europe a thousand years ago.

So did the people of those nations of Europe who received their kings and their government at the whim of the conquering Napoleon.

Whatever its new trappings and new slogans, tyranny is the oldest and most discredited rule known to history. And whenever tyranny has replaced a more human form of Government it has been due more to internal causes than external. Democracy can thrive only when it enlists the devotion of those whom Lincoln called the common people. Democracy can hold that devotion only when it adequately respects their dignity by so ordering society as to assure to the masses of men and women reasonable security and hope for themselves and for their children.

We in our democracy, and those who live in still unconquered democracies, will never willingly descend to any form of this so-called security of efficiency which calls for the abandonment of other securities more vital to the dignity of man. It is our credo — unshakable to the end — that we must live under the liberties that were first heralded by Magna Carta and placed into glorious operation through the Declaration of Independence, the Constitution of the United States and the Bill of Rights.

The Government of the United States for the past seven years has had the courage openly to oppose by every peaceful means the spread of the dictator form of Government. If our Government should pass to other hands next January — untried hands, inexperienced hands — we can merely hope and pray that they will not substitute appeasement and compromise with those who seek to destroy all democracies everywhere, including here.

I would not undo, if I could, the efforts I made to prevent war from the moment it was threatened and to restrict the area of carnage, down to the last minute. I do not now soften the condemnation expressed by Secretary Hull and myself from time to time for the acts of aggression that have wiped out ancient liberty-loving, peace-pursuing countries which had scrupulously maintained neutrality. I do not recant the sentiments of sympathy with all free peoples resisting such aggression, or begrudge the material aid that we have given to them. I do not regret my consistent endeavor to awaken this country to the menace for us and for all we hold dear.

I have pursued these efforts in the face of appeaser fifth columnists who charged me with hysteria and war-mongering. But I felt it my duty, my simple, plain, inescapable duty, to arouse my countrymen to the danger of the new forces let loose in the world.

So long as I am President, I will do all I can to insure that that foreign policy remain our foreign policy.

All that I have done to maintain the peace of this country and to prepare it morally, as well as physically, for whatever contingencies may be in store, I submit to the judgment of my countrymen. We face one of the great choices of history.

It is not alone a choice of Government by the people versus dictatorship.

It is not alone a choice of freedom versus slavery.

It is not alone a choice between moving forward or falling back. It is all of these rolled into one.

It is the continuance of civilization as we know it versus the ultimate destruction of all that we have held dear — religion against godlessness; the ideal of justice against the practice of force; moral decency versus the firing squad; courage to speak out, and to act, versus the false lullaby of appeasement.

But it has been well said that a selfish and greedy people cannot be free.

The American people must decide whether these things are worth making sacrifices of money, of energy, and of self. They will not decide by listening to mere words or by reading mere pledges, interpretations and claims. They will decide on the record — the record as it has been made — the record of things as they are.

The American people will sustain the progress of a representative democracy, asking the Divine Blessing as they face the future with courage and with faith.

Fireside Chat 16: On National Security

The "Arsenal of Democracy"

(December 29, 1940)

My friends:

This is not a fireside chat on war. It is a talk on national security, because the nub of the whole purpose of your President is to keep you now, and your children later, and your grandchildren much later, out of a last-ditch war for the preservation of American independence and all of the things that American independence means to you and to me and to ours.

Tonight, in the presence of a world crisis, my mind goes back eight years to a night in the midst of a domestic crisis. It was a time when the wheels of American industry were grinding to a full stop, when the whole banking system of our country had ceased to function.

I well remember that while I sat in my study in the White House, preparing to talk with the people of the United States, I had before my eyes the picture of all those Americans with whom I was talking. I saw the workmen in the mills, the mines, the factories; the girl behind the counter; the small shopkeeper; the farmer doing his spring plowing; the widows and the old men wondering about their life's savings.

I tried to convey to the great mass of American people what the banking crisis meant to them in their daily lives.

Tonight, I want to do the same thing, with the same people, in this new crisis which faces America.

We met the issue of 1933 with courage and realism.

We face this new crisis—this new threat to the security of our nation—with the same courage and realism.

Never before since Jamestown and Plymouth Rock has our American civilization been in such danger as now.

For, on September 27th, 1940, this year, by an agreement signed in Berlin, three powerful nations, two in Europe and one in Asia, joined themselves together in the threat that if the United States of America interfered with or blocked the expansion program of these three nations—a program aimed at world control—they would unite in ultimate action against the United States.

The Nazi masters of Germany have made it clear that they intend not only to dominate all life and thought in their own country, but also to enslave the whole of Europe, and then to use the resources of Europe to dominate the rest of the world.

It was only three weeks ago their leader stated this: " There are two worlds that stand opposed to each other." And then in defiant reply to his opponents, he said this: "Others are correct when they say: With this world we cannot ever reconcile ourselves .... I can beat any other power in the world." So said the leader of the Nazis.

In other words, the Axis not merely admits but the Axis proclaims that there can be no ultimate peace between their philosophy of government and our philosophy of government.

In view of the nature of this undeniable threat, it can be asserted, properly and categorically, that the United States has no right or reason to encourage talk of peace, until the day shall come when there is a clear intention on the part of the aggressor nations to abandon all thought of dominating or conquering the world.

At this moment, the forces of the states that are leagued against all peoples who live in freedom are being held away from our shores. The Germans and the Italians are being blocked on the other side of the Atlantic by the British, and by the Greeks, and by thousands of soldiers and sailors who were able to escape from subjugated countries. In Asia the Japanese are being engaged by the Chinese nation in another great defense.

In the Pacific Ocean is our fleet.

Some of our people like to believe that wars in Europe and in Asia are of no concern to us. But it is a matter of most vital concern to us that European and Asiatic war-makers should not gain control of the oceans which lead to this hemisphere.

One hundred and seventeen years ago the Monroe Doctrine was conceived by our Government as a measure of defense in the face of a threat against this hemisphere by an alliance in Continental Europe. Thereafter, we stood guard in the Atlantic, with the British as neighbors. There was no treaty. There was no "unwritten agreement."

And yet, there was the feeling, proven correct by history, that we as neighbors could settle any disputes in peaceful fashion. And the fact is that during the whole of this time the Western Hemisphere has remained free from aggression from Europe or from Asia.

Does anyone seriously believe that we need to fear attack anywhere in the Americas while a free Britain remains our most powerful naval neighbor in the Atlantic? And does anyone seriously believe, on the other hand, that we could rest easy if the Axis powers were our neighbors there?

If Great Britain goes down, the Axis powers will control the continents of Europe, Asia, Africa, Australia, and the high seas — and they will be in a position to bring enormous military and naval resources against this hemisphere. It is no exaggeration to say that all of us, in all the Americas, would be living at the point of a gun — a gun loaded with explosive bullets, economic as well as military.

We should enter upon a new and terrible era in which the whole world, our hemisphere included, would be run by threats of brute force. And to survive in such a world, we would have to convert ourselves permanently into a militaristic power on the basis of war economy.

Some of us like to believe that even if Britain falls, we are still safe, because of the broad expanse of the Atlantic and of the Pacific.

But the width of those oceans is not what it was in the days of clipper ships. At one point between Africa and Brazil the distance is less from Washington than it is from Washington to Denver, Colorado — five hours for the latest type of bomber. And at the North end of the Pacific Ocean America and Asia almost touch each other.

Why, even today we have planes that could fly from the British Isles to New England and back again without refueling. And remember that the range of a modern bomber is ever being increased.

During the past week many people in all parts of the nation have told me what they wanted me to say tonight. Almost all of them expressed a courageous desire to hear the plain truth about the gravity of the situation. One telegram, however, expressed the attitude of the small minority who want to see no evil and hear no evil, even though they know in their hearts that evil exists. That telegram begged me not to tell again of the ease with which our American cities could be bombed by any hostile power which had gained bases in this Western Hemisphere. The gist of that telegram was: "Please, Mr. President, don't frighten us by telling us the facts."

Frankly and definitely there is danger ahead—danger against which we must prepare. But we well know that we cannot escape danger, or the fear of danger, by crawling into bed and pulling the covers over our heads.

Some nations of Europe were bound by solemn non-intervention pacts with Germany. Other nations were assured by Germany that they need never fear invasion. Non-intervention pact or not, the fact remains that they were attacked, overrun, thrown into modern slavery at an hour's notice, or even without any notice at all. As an exiled leader of one of these nations said to me the other day, "The notice was a minus quantity. It was given to my Government two hours after German troops had poured into my country in a hundred places."

The fate of these nations tells us what it means to live at the point of a Nazi gun.

The Nazis have justified such actions by various pious frauds. One of these frauds is the claim that they are occupying a nation for the purpose of "restoring order." Another is that they are occupying or controlling a nation on the excuse that they are "protecting it" against the aggression of somebody else.

For example, Germany has said that she was occupying Belgium to save the Belgians from the British. Would she then hesitate to say to any South American country, "We are occupying you to protect you from aggression by the United States?"

Belgium today is being used as an invasion base against Britain, now fighting for its life. And any South American country, in Nazi hands, would always constitute a jumping-off place for German attack on any one of the other republics of this hemisphere.

Analyze for yourselves the future of two other places even nearer to Germany if the Nazis won. Could Ireland hold out?

Would Irish freedom be permitted as an amazing pet exception in an unfree world? Or the Islands of the Azores which still fly the flag of Portugal after five centuries? You and I think of Hawaii as an outpost of defense in the Pacific. And yet, the Azores are closer to our shores in the Atlantic than Hawaii is on the other side.

There are those who say that the Axis powers would never have any desire to attack the Western Hemisphere. That is the same dangerous form of wishful thinking which has destroyed the powers of resistance of so many conquered peoples. The plain facts are that the Nazis have proclaimed, time and again, that all other races are their inferiors and therefore subject to their orders. And most important of all, the vast resources and wealth of this American Hemisphere constitute the most tempting loot in all of the round world.

Let us no longer blind ourselves to the undeniable fact that the evil forces which have crushed and undermined and corrupted so many others are already within our own gates. Your Government knows much about them and every day is ferreting them out.

Their secret emissaries are active in our own and in neighboring countries. They seek to stir up suspicion and dissension to cause internal strife. They try to turn capital against labor, and vice versa. They try to reawaken long slumbering racist and religious enmities which should have no place in this country. They are active in every group that promotes intolerance. They exploit for their own ends our own natural abhorrence of war. These trouble-breeders have but one purpose. It is to divide our people, to divide them into hostile groups and to destroy our unity and shatter our will to defend ourselves.

There are also American citizens, many of then in high places, who, unwittingly in most cases, are aiding and abetting the work of these agents. I do not charge these American citizens with being foreign agents. But I do charge them with doing exactly the kind of work that the dictators want done in the United States.

These people not only believe that we can save our own skins by shutting our eyes to the fate of other nations. Some of them go much further than that. They say that we can and should become the friends and even the partners of the Axis powers. Some of them even suggest that we should imitate the methods of the dictatorships. But Americans never can and never will do that.

The experience of the past two years has proven beyond doubt that no nation can appease the Nazis. No man can tame a tiger into a kitten by stroking it. There can be no appeasement with ruthlessness. There can be no reasoning with an incendiary bomb. We know now that a nation can have peace with the Nazis only at the price of total surrender.

Even the people of Italy have been forced to become accomplices of the Nazis, but at this moment they do not know how soon they will be embraced to death by their allies.

The American appeasers ignore the warning to be found in the fate of Austria, Czechoslovakia, Poland, Norway, Belgium, the Netherlands, Denmark and France. They tell you that the Axis powers are going to win anyway; that all of this bloodshed in the world could be saved, that the United States might just as well throw its influence into the scale of a dictated peace, and get the best out of it that we can.

They call it a "negotiated peace." Nonsense! Is it a negotiated peace if a gang of outlaws surrounds your community and on threat of extermination makes you pay tribute to save your own skins?

Such a dictated peace would be no peace at all. It would be only another armistice, leading to the most gigantic armament race and the most devastating trade wars in all history. And in these contests the Americas would offer the only real resistance to the Axis powers.

With all their vaunted efficiency, with all their parade of pious purpose in this war, there are still in their background the concentration camp and the servants of God in chains.

The history of recent years proves that the shootings and the chains and the concentration camps are not simply the transient tools but the very altars of modern dictatorships. They may talk of a "new order" in the world, but what they have in mind is only a revival of the oldest and the worst tyranny. In that there is no liberty, no religion, no hope.

The proposed "new order" is the very opposite of a United States of Europe or a United States of Asia. It is not a government based upon the consent of the governed. It is not a union of ordinary, self-respecting men and women to protect themselves and their freedom and their dignity from oppression. It is an unholy alliance of power and pelf to dominate and to enslave the human race.

The British people and their allies today are conducting an active war against this unholy alliance. Our own future security is greatly dependent on the outcome of that fight. Our ability to "keep out of war" is going to be affected by that outcome.

Thinking in terms of today and tomorrow, I make the direct statement to the American people that there is far less chance of the United States getting into war if we do all we can now to support the nations defending themselves against attack by the Axis than if we acquiesce in their defeat, submit tamely to an Axis victory, and wait our turn to be the object of attack in another war later on.

If we are to be completely honest with ourselves, we must admit that there is risk in any course we may take. But I deeply believe that the great majority of our people agree that the course that I advocate involves the least risk now and the greatest hope for world peace in the future.

The people of Europe who are defending themselves do not ask us to do their fighting. They ask us for the implements of war, the planes, the tanks, the guns, the freighters which will enable them to fight for their liberty and for our security. Emphatically we must get these weapons to them, get them to them in sufficient volume and quickly enough, so that we and our children will be saved the agony and suffering of war which others have had to endure.

Let not the defeatists tell us that it is too late. It will never be earlier. Tomorrow will be later than today.

Certain facts are self-evident.

In a military sense Great Britain and the British Empire are today the spearhead of resistance to world conquest. And they are putting up a fight which will live forever in the story of human gallantry.

There is no demand for sending an American Expeditionary Force outside our own borders. There is no intention by any member of your Government to send such a force. You can, therefore, nail — nail any talk about sending armies to Europe as deliberate untruth.

Our national policy is not directed toward war. Its sole purpose is to keep war away from our country and away from our people.

Democracy's fight against world conquest is being greatly aided, and must be more greatly aided, by the rearmament of the United States and by sending every ounce and every ton of munitions and supplies that we can possibly spare to help the defenders who are in the front lines. And it is no more unneutral for us to do that than it is for Sweden, Russia and other nations near Germany to send steel and ore and oil and other war materials into Germany every day in the week.

We are planning our own defense with the utmost urgency, and in its vast scale we must integrate the war needs of Britain and the other free nations which are resisting aggression.

This is not a matter of sentiment or of controversial personal opinion. It is a matter of realistic, practical military policy, based on the advice of our military experts who are in close touch with existing warfare. These military and naval experts and the members of the Congress and the Administration have a single-minded purpose — the defense of the United States.

This nation is making a great effort to produce everything that is necessary in this emergency — and with all possible speed. And this great effort requires great sacrifice.

I would ask no one to defend a democracy which in turn would not defend everyone in the nation against want and privation. The strength of this nation shall not be diluted by the failure of the Government to protect the economic well-being of its citizens.

If our capacity to produce is limited by machines, it must ever be remembered that these machines are operated by the skill and the stamina of the workers. As the Government is determined to protect the rights of the workers, so the nation has a right to expect that the men who man the machines will discharge their full responsibilities to the urgent needs of defense.

The worker possesses the same human dignity and is entitled to the same security of position as the engineer or the manager or the owner. For the workers provide the human power that turns out the destroyers, and the planes and the tanks.

The nation expects our defense industries to continue operation without interruption by strikes or lockouts. It expects and insists that management and workers will reconcile their differences by voluntary or legal means, to continue to produce the supplies that are so sorely needed.

And on the economic side of our great defense program, we are, as you know, bending every effort to maintain stability of prices and with that the stability of the cost of living.

Nine days ago I announced the setting up of a more effective organization to direct our gigantic efforts to increase the production of munitions. The appropriation of vast sums of money and a well coordinated executive direction of our defense efforts are not in themselves enough. Guns, planes, ships and many other things have to be built in the factories and the arsenals of America. They have to be produced by workers and managers and engineers with the aid of machines which in turn have to be built by hundreds of thousands of workers throughout the land.

In this great work there has been splendid cooperation between the Government and industry and labor, and I am very thankful.

American industrial genius, unmatched throughout all the world in the solution of production problems, has been called upon to bring its resources and its talents into action. Manufacturers of watches, of farm implements, of linotypes, and cash registers, and automobiles, and sewing machines, and lawn mowers and locomotives are now making fuses, bomb packing crates, telescope mounts, shells, and pistols and tanks.

But all of our present efforts are not enough. We must have more ships, more guns, more planes — more of everything. And this can only be accomplished if we discard the notion of "business as usual." This job cannot be done merely by superimposing on the existing productive facilities the added requirements of the nation for defense.

Our defense efforts must not be blocked by those who fear the future consequences of surplus plant capacity. The possible consequences of failure of our defense efforts now are much more to be feared.

And after the present needs of our defense are past, a proper handling of the country's peacetime needs will require all of the new productive capacity — if not still more.

No pessimistic policy about the future of America shall delay the immediate expansion of those industries essential to defense. We need them.

I want to make it clear that it is the purpose of the nation to build now with all possible speed every machine, every arsenal, every factory that we need to manufacture our defense material. We have the men—the skill—the wealth—and above all, the will.

I am confident that if and when production of consumer or luxury goods in certain industries requires the use of machines and raw materials that are essential for defense purposes, then such production must yield, and will gladly yield, to our primary and compelling purpose.

So I appeal to the owners of plants—to the managers -to the workers—to our own Government employees—to put every ounce of effort into producing these munitions swiftly and without stint. With this appeal I give you the pledge that all of us who are officers of your Government will devote ourselves to the same whole-hearted extent to the great task that lies ahead.

As planes and ships and guns and shells are produced, your Government, with its defense experts, can then determine how best to use them to defend this hemisphere. The decision as to how much shall be sent abroad and how much shall remain at home must be made on the basis of our overall military necessities.

We must be the great arsenal of democracy. For us this is an emergency as serious as war itself. We must apply ourselves to our task with the same resolution, the same sense of urgency, the same spirit of patriotism and sacrifice as we would show were we at war.

We have furnished the British great material support and we will furnish far more in the future. There will be no "bottlenecks" in our determination to aid Great Britain. No dictator, no combination of dictators, will weaken that determination by threats of how they will construe that determination.

The British have received invaluable military support from the heroic Greek army and from the forces of all the governments in exile. Their strength is growing. It is the strength of men and women who value their freedom more highly than they value their lives.

I believe that the Axis powers are not going to win this war. I base that belief on the latest and best of information.

We have no excuse for defeatism. We have every good reason for hope—hope for peace, yes, and hope for the defense of our civilization and for the building of a better civilization in the future.

I have the profound conviction that the American people are now determined to put forth a mightier effort than they have ever yet made to increase our production of all the implements of defense, to meet the threat to our democratic faith.

As President of the United States I call for that national effort. I call for it in the name of this nation which we love and honor and which we are privileged and proud to serve. I call upon our people with absolute confidence that our common cause will greatly succeed.

State of the Union

The "Four Freedoms" Speech

(January 6, 1941)

Mr. President, Mr. Speaker, Members of the Seventy-seventh Congress:

I address you, the Members of the Seventy-seventh Congress, at a moment unprecedented in the history of the Union. I use the word "unprecedented," because at no previous time has American security been as seriously threatened from without as it is today.

Since the permanent formation of our Government under the Constitution, in 1789, most of the periods of crisis in our history have related to our domestic affairs. Fortunately, only one of these — the four-year War Between the States — ever threatened our national unity. Today, thank God, one hundred and thirty million Americans, in forty-eight States, have forgotten points of the compass in our national unity.

It is true that prior to 1914 the United States often had been disturbed by events in other Continents. We had even engaged in two wars with European nations and in a number of undeclared wars in the West Indies, in the Mediterranean and in the Pacific for the maintenance of American rights and for the principles of peaceful commerce. But in no case had a serious threat been raised against our national safety or our continued independence.

What I seek to convey is the historic truth that the United States as a nation has at all times maintained clear, definite opposition, to any attempt to lock us in behind an ancient Chinese wall while the procession of civilization went past. Today, thinking of our children and of their children, we oppose enforced isolation for ourselves or for any other part of the Americas.

That determination of ours, extending over all these years, was proved, for example, during the quarter century of wars following the French Revolution.

While the Napoleonic struggles did threaten interests of the United States because of the French foothold in the West Indies and in Louisiana, and while we engaged in the War of 1812 to vindicate our right to peaceful trade, it is nevertheless clear that neither France nor Great Britain, nor any other nation, was aiming at domination of the whole world.

In like fashion from 1815 to 1914 — ninety-nine years — no single war in Europe or in Asia constituted a real threat against our future or against the future of any other American nation.

Except in the Maximilian interlude in Mexico, no foreign power sought to establish itself in this Hemisphere; and the strength of the British fleet in the Atlantic has been a friendly strength. It is still a friendly strength.

Even when the World War broke out in 1914, it seemed to contain only small threat of danger to our own American future. But, as time went on, the American people began to visualize what the downfall of democratic nations might mean to our own democracy.

We need not overemphasize imperfections in the Peace of Versailles. We need not harp on failure of the democracies to deal with problems of world reconstruction. We should remember that the Peace of 1919 was far less unjust than the kind of "pacification" which began even before Munich, and which is being carried on under the new order of tyranny that seeks to spread over every continent today. The American people have unalterably set their faces against that tyranny.

Every realist knows that the democratic way of life is at this moment being directly assailed in every part of the world — assailed either by arms, or by secret spreading of poisonous propaganda by those who seek to destroy unity and promote discord in nations that are still at peace.

During sixteen long months this assault has blotted out the whole pattern of democratic life in an appalling number of independent nations, great and small. The assailants are still on the march, threatening other nations, great and small.

Therefore, as your President, performing my constitutional duty to "give to the Congress information of the state of the Union," I find it, unhappily, necessary to report that the future and the safety of our country and of our democracy are overwhelmingly involved in events far beyond our borders.

Armed defense of democratic existence is now being gallantly waged in four continents. If that defense fails, all the population and all the resources of Europe, Asia, Africa, and Australasia will be dominated by the conquerors. Let us remember that the total of those populations and their resources in those four continents greatly exceeds the sum total of the population and the resources of the whole of the Western Hemisphere — many times over.

In times like these it is immature — and incidentally, untrue — for anybody to brag that an unprepared America, single-handed, and with one hand tied behind its back, can hold off the whole world.

No realistic American can expect from a dictator's peace international generosity, or return of true independence, or world disarmament, or freedom of expression, or freedom of religion, or even good business.

Such a peace would bring no security for us or for our neighbors. "Those, who would give up essential liberty to purchase a little temporary safety, deserve neither liberty nor safety."

As a nation, we may take pride in the fact that we are softhearted; but we cannot afford to be soft-headed.

We must always be wary of those who with sounding brass and a tinkling cymbal preach the "ism" of appeasement.

We must especially beware of that small group of selfish men who would clip the wings of the American eagle in order to feather their own nests.

I have recently pointed out how quickly the tempo of modern warfare could bring into our very midst the physical attack which we must eventually expect if the dictator nations win this war.

There is much loose talk of our immunity from immediate and direct invasion from across the seas. Obviously, as long as the British Navy retains its power, no such danger exists. Even if there were no British Navy, it is not probable that any enemy would be stupid enough to attack us by landing troops in the United States from across thousands of miles of ocean, until it had acquired strategic bases from which to operate.

But we learn much from the lessons of the past years in Europe — particularly the lesson of Norway, whose essential seaports were captured by treachery and surprise built up over a series of years.

The first phase of the invasion of this Hemisphere would not be the landing of regular troops. The necessary strategic points would be occupied by secret agents and their dupes—and great numbers of them are already here, and in Latin America.

As long as the aggressor nations maintain the offensive, they—not we—will choose the time and the place and the method of their attack.

That is why the future of all the American Republics is today in serious danger.

That is why this Annual Message to the Congress is unique in our history.

That is why every member of the Executive Branch of the Government and every member of the Congress faces great responsibility and great accountability.

The need of the moment is that our actions and our policy should be devoted primarily—almost exclusively—to meeting this foreign peril. For all our domestic problems are now a part of the great emergency.

Just as our national policy in internal affairs has been based upon a decent respect for the rights and the dignity of all our fellow men within our gates, so our national policy in foreign affairs has been based on a decent respect for the rights and dignity of all nations, large and small. And the justice of morality must and will win in the end.

Our national policy is this:

First, by an impressive expression of the public will and without regard to partisanship, we are committed to all-inclusive national defense.

Second, by an impressive expression of the public will and without regard to partisanship, we are committed to full support of all those resolute peoples, everywhere, who are resisting aggression and are thereby keeping war away from our Hemisphere. By this support, we express our determination that the democratic cause shall prevail; and we strengthen the defense and the security of our own nation.

Third, by an impressive expression of the public will and without regard to partisanship, we are committed to the proposition that principles of morality and considerations for our own security will never permit us to acquiesce in a peace dictated by aggressors and sponsored by appeasers. We know that enduring peace cannot be bought at the cost of other people's freedom.

In the recent national election there was no substantial difference between the two great parties in respect to that national policy. No issue was fought out on this line before the American electorate. Today it is abundantly evident that American citizens everywhere are demanding and supporting speedy and complete action in recognition of obvious danger.

Therefore, the immediate need is a swift and driving increase in our armament production.

Leaders of industry and labor have responded to our summons. Goals of speed have been set. In some cases these goals are being reached ahead of time; in some cases we are on schedule; in other cases there are slight but not serious delays; and in some cases—and I am sorry to say very important cases—we are all concerned by the slowness of the accomplishment of our plans.

The Army and Navy, however, have made substantial progress during the past year. Actual experience is improving and speeding up our methods of production with every passing day. And today's best is not good enough for tomorrow.

I am not satisfied with the progress thus far made. The men in charge of the program represent the best in training, in ability, and in patriotism. They are not satisfied with the progress thus far made. None of us will be satisfied until the job is done.

No matter whether the original goal was set too high or too low, our objective is quicker and better results. To give you two illustrations:

We are behind schedule in turning out finished airplanes; we are working day and night to solve the innumerable problems and to catch up.

We are ahead of schedule in building warships but we are working to get even further ahead of that schedule.

To change a whole nation from a basis of peacetime production of implements of peace to a basis of wartime production of implements of war is no small task. And the greatest difficulty comes at the beginning of the program, when new tools, new plant facilities, new assembly lines, and new ship ways must first be constructed before the actual materiel begins to flow steadily and speedily from them.

The Congress, of course, must rightly keep itself informed at all times of the progress of the program. However, there is certain information, as the Congress itself will readily recognize, which, in the interests of our own security and those of the nations that we are supporting, must of needs be kept in confidence.

New circumstances are constantly begetting new needs for our safety. I shall ask this Congress for greatly increased new appropriations and authorizations to carry on what we have begun.

I also ask this Congress for authority and for funds sufficient to manufacture additional munitions and war supplies of many kinds, to be turned over to those nations which are now in actual war with aggressor nations.

Our most useful and immediate role is to act as an arsenal for them as well as for ourselves. They do not need man power, but they do need billions of dollars worth of the weapons of defense.

The time is near when they will not be able to pay for them all in ready cash. We cannot, and we will not, tell them that they must surrender, merely because of present inability to pay for the weapons which we know they must have.

I do not recommend that we make them a loan of dollars with which to pay for these weapons—a loan to be repaid in dollars.

I recommend that we make it possible for those nations to continue to obtain war materials in the United States, fitting their orders into our own program. Nearly all their materiel would, if the time ever came, be useful for our own defense.

Taking counsel of expert military and naval authorities, considering what is best for our own security, we are free to decide how much should be kept here and how much should be sent abroad to our friends who by their determined and heroic resistance are giving us time in which to make ready our own defense.

For what we send abroad, we shall be repaid within a reasonable time following the close of hostilities, in similar materials, or, at our option, in other goods of many kinds, which they can produce and which we need.

Let us say to the democracies: "We Americans are vitally concerned in your defense of freedom. We are putting forth our energies, our resources and our organizing powers to give you the strength to regain and maintain a free world. We shall send you, in ever-increasing numbers, ships, planes, tanks, guns. This is our purpose and our pledge."

In fulfillment of this purpose we will not be intimidated by the threats of dictators that they will regard as a breach of international law or as an act of war our aid to the democracies which dare to resist their aggression. Such aid is not an act of war, even if a dictator should unilaterally proclaim it so to be.

When the dictators, if the dictators, are ready to make war upon us, they will not wait for an act of war on our part. They did not wait for Norway or Belgium or the Netherlands to commit an act of war.

Their only interest is in a new one-way international law, which lacks mutuality in its observance, and, therefore, becomes an instrument of oppression.

The happiness of future generations of Americans may well depend upon how effective and how immediate we can make our aid felt. No one can tell the exact character of the emergency situations that we may be called upon to meet. The Nation's hands must not be tied when the Nation's life is in danger.

We must all prepare to make the sacrifices that the emergency—almost as serious as war itself—demands. Whatever stands in the way of speed and efficiency in defense preparations must give way to the national need.

A free nation has the right to expect full cooperation from all groups. A free nation has the right to look to the leaders of business, of labor, and of agriculture to take the lead in stimulating effort, not among other groups but within their own groups.

The best way of dealing with the few slackers or trouble makers in our midst is, first, to shame them by patriotic example, and, if that fails, to use the sovereignty of Government to save Government.

As men do not live by bread alone, they do not fight by armaments alone. Those who man our defenses, and those behind them who build our defenses, must have the stamina and the courage which come from unshakable belief in the manner of life which they are defending. The mighty action that we are calling for cannot be based on a disregard of all things worth fighting for.

The Nation takes great satisfaction and much strength from the things which have been done to make its people conscious of their individual stake in the preservation of democratic life in America. Those things have toughened the fibre of our people, have renewed their faith and strengthened their devotion to the institutions we make ready to protect.

Certainly this is no time for any of us to stop thinking about the social and economic problems which are the root cause of the social revolution which is today a supreme factor in the world.

For there is nothing mysterious about the foundations of a healthy and strong democracy. The basic things expected by our people of their political and economic systems are simple. They are:

Equality of opportunity for youth and for others.

Jobs for those who can work.

Security for those who need it.

The ending of special privilege for the few.

The preservation of civil liberties for all.

The enjoyment of the fruits of scientific progress in a wider and constantly rising standard of living.

These are the simple, basic things that must never be lost sight of in the turmoil and unbelievable complexity of our modern world. The inner and abiding strength of our economic and political systems is dependent upon the degree to which they fulfill these expectations.

Many subjects connected with our social economy call for immediate improvement. As examples:

We should bring more citizens under the coverage of old-age pensions and unemployment insurance.

We should widen the opportunities for adequate medical care.

We should plan a better system by which persons deserving or needing gainful employment may obtain it.

I have called for personal sacrifice. I am assured of the willingness of almost all Americans to respond to that call.

A part of the sacrifice means the payment of more money in taxes. In my Budget Message I shall recommend that a greater portion of this great defense program be paid for from taxation than we are paying today. No person should try, or be allowed, to get rich out of this program; and the principle of tax payments in accordance with ability to pay should be constantly before our eyes to guide our legislation.

If the Congress maintains these principles, the voters, putting patriotism ahead of pocketbooks, will give you their applause.

In the future days, which we seek to make secure, we look forward to a world founded upon four essential human freedoms.

The first is freedom of speech and expression—everywhere in the world.

The second is freedom of every person to worship God in his own way—everywhere in the world.

The third is freedom from want—which, translated into world terms, means economic understandings which will secure to every nation a healthy peacetime life for its inhabitants—everywhere in the world.

The fourth is freedom from fear—which, translated into world terms, means a world-wide reduction of armaments to such a point and in such a thorough fashion that no nation will be in a position to commit an act of physical aggression against any neighbor—anywhere in the world.

That is no vision of a distant millennium. It is a definite basis for a kind of world attainable in our own time and generation. That kind of world is the very antithesis of the so-called new order of tyranny which the dictators seek to create with the crash of a bomb.

To that new order we oppose the greater conception—the moral order. A good society is able to face schemes of world domination and foreign revolutions alike without fear.

Since the beginning of our American history, we have been engaged in change—in a perpetual peaceful revolution—a revolution which goes on steadily, quietly adjusting itself to changing conditions—without the concentration camp or the quick-lime in the ditch. The world order which we seek is the cooperation of free countries, working together in a friendly, civilized society.

This nation has placed its destiny in the hands and heads and hearts of its millions of free men and women; and its faith in freedom under the guidance of God. Freedom means the supremacy of human rights everywhere. Our support goes to those who struggle to gain those rights or keep them. Our strength is our unity of purpose. To that high concept there can be no end save victory.

Address at the White House Correspondents Association Dinner

Land Lease

(March 15, 1941)

This dinner of the White House Correspondents' Association is unique. It is the first one at which I have made a speech in all these eight years. It differs from the press conferences that you and I hold twice a week, for you cannot ask me any questions tonight; and everything that I have to say is word for word "on the record."

For eight years you and I have been helping each other. I have been trying to keep you informed of the news of Washington, of the Nation, and of the world, from the point of view of the Presidency. You, more than you realize, have been giving me a great deal of information about what the people of this country are thinking and saying.

In our press conferences, as at this dinner tonight, we include reporters representing papers and news agencies of many other lands. To most of them it is a matter of constant amazement that press conferences such as ours can exist in any Nation in the world.

That is especially true in those lands where freedoms do not exist—where the purposes of our democracy and the characteristics of our country and of our people have been seriously distorted.

Such misunderstandings are not new. I remember that, a quarter of a century ago, in the early days of the first World War, the German Government received solemn assurances from their representatives in the United States that the people of America were disunited; that they cared more for peace at any price than for the preservation of ideals and freedom; that there would even be riots and revolutions in the United States if this Nation ever asserted its own interests.

Let not dictators of Europe or Asia doubt our unanimity now. Before the present war broke out on September 1, 1939, I was more worried about the future than many people—indeed, than most people. The record shows that I was not worried enough.

That, however, is water over the dam. Do not let us waste time in reviewing the past, or fixing or dodging the blame for it. History cannot be rewritten by wishful thinking. We, the American people, are writing new history today.

The big news story of this week is this: The world has been told that we, as a united Nation, realize the danger that confronts us—and that to meet that danger our democracy has gone into action.

We know that although Prussian autocracy was bad enough in the first war, Nazism is far worse in this.

Nazi forces are not seeking mere modifications in colonial maps or in minor European boundaries. They openly seek the destruction of all elective systems of government on every continent—including our own; they seek to establish systems of government based on the regimentation of all human beings by a handful of individual rulers who have seized power by force.

Yes, these men and their hypnotized followers call this a new order. It is not new and it is not order. For order among Nations presupposes something enduring—some system of justice under which individuals, over a long period of time, are willing to live. Humanity will never permanently accept a system imposed by conquest and based on slavery.

These modern tyrants find it necessary to—their plans to eliminate all democracies—eliminate them one by one. The Nations of Europe, and indeed we ourselves, did not appreciate that purpose. We do now. The process of the elimination of the European Nations proceeded according to plan through 1939 and well into 1940, until the schedule was shot to pieces by the unbeatable defenders of Britain.

The enemies of democracy were wrong in their calculations for a very simple reason. They were wrong because they believed that democracy could not adjust itself to the terrible reality of a world at war.

They believed that democracy, because of its profound respect for the rights of man, would never arm itself to fight.

They believed that democracy, because of its will to live at peace with its neighbors, could not mobilize its energies even in its own defense.

They know now that democracy can still remain democracy, and speak, and reach conclusions, and arm itself adequately for defense.

From the bureaus of propaganda of the Axis powers came the confident prophecy that the conquest of our country would be "an inside job"—a job accomplished not by overpowering invasion from without, but by disrupting confusion and disunion and moral disintegration from within.

Those who believed that knew little of our history. America is not a country which can be confounded by the appeasers, the defeatists, the backstairs manufacturers of panic. It is a country that talks out its problems in the open, where any man can hear them.

We have just now engaged in a great debate. It was not limited to the halls of Congress. It was argued in every newspaper, on every wave length, over every cracker barrel in all the land; and it was finally settled and decided by the American people themselves.

Yes, the decisions of our democracy may be slowly arrived at. But when that decision is made, it is proclaimed not with the voice of any one man but with the voice of one hundred and thirty millions. It is binding on us all. And the world is no longer left in doubt.

This decision is the end of any attempts at appeasement in our land; the end of urging us to get along with dictators; the end of compromise with tyranny and the forces of oppression.

And the urgency is now.

We believe firmly that when our production output is in full swing, the democracies of the world will be able to prove that dictatorships cannot win.

But, now, now, the time element is of supreme importance. Every plane, every other instrument of war, old and new, every instrument that we can spare now, we will send overseas because that is the common sense of strategy.

The great task of this day, the deep duty that rests upon each and every one of us is to move products from the assembly lines of our factories to the battle lines of democracy—Now!

We can have speed, we can have effectiveness, if we maintain our existing unity. We do not have and never will have the false unity of a people browbeaten by threats, misled by propaganda. Ours is a unity that is possible only among free men and women who recognize the truth and face reality with intelligence and courage.

Today, at last—today at long last—ours is not a partial effort. It is a total effort and that is the only way to guarantee ultimate safety.

Beginning a year ago, we started the erection of hundreds of plants; we started the training of millions of men.

Then, at the moment that the aid-to-democracies bill was passed, this week, we were ready to recommend the seven-billion-dollar appropriation on the basis of capacity production as now planned.

The articles themselves cover the whole range of munitions of war and of the facilities for transporting them across the seas.

The aid-to-democracies bill was agreed on by both houses of the Congress last Tuesday afternoon. I signed it one half hour later. Five minutes after that I approved a list of articles for immediate shipment; and today—Saturday night—many of them are on their way. On Wednesday, I recommended an appropriation for new material to the extent of seven billion dollars; and the Congress is making patriotic speed in making the money available.

Here in Washington, we are thinking in terms of speed and speed now. And I hope that that watchword—"Speed, and speed now"—will find its way into every home in the Nation.

We shall have to make sacrifices—every one of us. The final extent of those sacrifices will depend on the speed with which we act *Now!*

I must tell you tonight in plain language what this undertaking means to you—to you in your daily life.

Whether you are in the armed services; whether you are a steel worker or a stevedore; a machinist or a housewife; a farmer or a banker; a storekeeper or a manufacturer—to all of you it will mean sacrifice in behalf of your country and your liberties. Yes, you will feel the impact of this gigantic effort in your daily lives. You will feel it in a way that will cause, to you, many inconveniences.

You will have to be content with lower profits, lower profits from business because obviously your taxes will be higher.

You will have to work longer at your bench, or your plow, or your machine, or your desk.

Let me make it clear that the Nation is calling for the sacrifice of some privileges, not for the sacrifice of fundamental rights. And most of us will do it willingly. That kind of sacrifice is for the common national protection and welfare; for our defense against the most ruthless brutality in all history; for the ultimate victory of a way of life now so violently menaced.

A halfhearted effort on our part will lead to failure. This is no part-time job. The concepts of "business as usual," of "normalcy," must be forgotten until the task is finished. Yes, it's an all-out effort—and nothing short of an all-out effort will win.

Therefore, we are dedicated, from here on, to a constantly increasing tempo of production—a production greater than we now know or have ever known before—a production that does not stop and should not pause.

Tonight, I am appealing to the heart and to the mind of every man and every woman within our borders who loves liberty. I ask you to consider the needs of our Nation and this hour, to put aside all personal differences until the victory is won.

The light of democracy must be kept burning. To the perpetuation of this light, each of us must do his own share. The single effort of one individual may seem very small. But there are 130 million individuals over here. And there are many more millions in Britain and elsewhere bravely shielding the great flame of democracy from the blackout of barbarism. It is not enough for us merely to trim the wick, or polish the glass. The time has come when we must provide the fuel in ever-increasing amounts to keep that flame alight.

There will be no divisions of party or section or race or nationality or religion. There is not one among us who does not have a stake in the outcome of the effort in which we are now engaged.

A few weeks ago I spoke of four freedoms — freedom of speech and expression, freedom of every person to worship God in his own way, freedom from want, freedom from fear. They are the ultimate stake. They may not be immediately attainable throughout the world but humanity does move toward those glorious ideals through democratic processes. And if we fail — if democracy is superseded by slavery — then those four freedoms, or even the mention of them, will become forbidden things. Centuries will pass before they can be revived.

By winning now, we strengthen the meaning of those freedoms, we increase the stature of mankind, we establish the dignity of human life.

I have often thought that there is a vast difference between the word "loyalty" and the word "obedience." Obedience can be obtained and enforced in a dictatorship by the use of threat or extortion or blackmail or it can be obtained by a failure on the part of government to tell the truth to its citizens.

Loyalty is different. It springs from the mind that is given the facts, that retains ancient ideals and proceeds without coercion to give support to its own government.

That is true in England and in Greece and in China and in the United States, today. And in many other countries millions of men and women are praying for the return of a day when they can give that kind of loyalty.

Loyalty cannot be bought. Dollars alone will not win this war. Let us not delude ourselves as to that.

Today, nearly a million and a half American citizens are hard at work in our armed forces. The spirit — the determination of these men of our Army and Navy are worthy of the highest traditions of our country. No better men ever served under Washington or John Paul Jones or Grant or Lee or Pershing. That is a boast, I admit, but it is not an idle one.

Upon the national will to sacrifice and to work depends the output of our industry and our agriculture.

Upon that will depends the survival of the vital bridge across the ocean—the bridge of ships that carry the arms and the food for those who are fighting the good fight.

Upon that will depends our ability to aid other Nations which may determine to offer resistance.

Upon that will may depend practical assistance to people now living in Nations that have been overrun, should they find the opportunity to strike back in an effort to regain their liberties and may that day come soon!

This will of the American people will not be frustrated, either by threats from powerful enemies abroad or by small, selfish groups or individuals at home.

The determination of America must not and will not be obstructed by war profiteering.

It must not be obstructed by unnecessary strikes of workers, by shortsighted management, or by the third danger—deliberate sabotage.

For, unless we win there will be no freedom for either management or labor.

Wise labor leaders and wise business managers will realize how necessary it is to their own existence to make common sacrifice for this great common cause.

There is no longer the slightest question or doubt that the American people recognize the extreme seriousness of the present situation. That is why they have demanded, and got, a policy of unqualified, immediate, all-out aid for Britain, for Greece, for China, and for all the Governments in exile whose homelands are temporarily occupied by the aggressors.

And from now on that aid will be increased—and yet again increased—until total victory has been won.

The British are stronger than ever in the magnificent morale that has enabled them to endure all the dark days and the shattered nights of the past ten months. They have the full support and help of Canada, of the other Dominions, of the rest of their Empire, and the full aid and support of non-British people throughout the world who still think in terms of the great freedoms.

The British people are braced for invasion whenever such attempt may come — tomorrow — next week — next month.

In this historic crisis, Britain is blessed with a brilliant and great leader in Winston Churchill. But, knowing him, no one knows better than Mr. Churchill himself that it is not alone his stirring words and valiant deeds that give the British their superb morale. The essence of that morale is in the masses of plain people who are completely clear in their minds about the one essential fact — that they would rather die as free men than live as slaves.

These plain people — civilians as well as soldiers and sailors and airmen — women and girls as well as men and boys — they are fighting in the front line of civilization at this moment, and they are holding that line with a fortitude that will forever be the pride and the inspiration of all free men on every continent, on every isle of the sea.

The British people and their Grecian allies need ships. From America, they will get ships.

They need planes. From America, they will get planes.

From America they need food. From America, they will get food.

They need tanks and guns and ammunition and supplies of all kinds. From America, they will get tanks and guns and ammunition and supplies of all kinds.

China likewise expresses the magnificent will of millions of plain people to resist the dismemberment of their historic

Nation. China, through the Generalissimo, Chiang Kai-shek, asks our help. America has said that China shall have our help.

And so our country is going to be what our people have proclaimed it must be — the arsenal of democracy.

Our country is going to play its full part.

And when — no, I didn't say if, I said when — dictatorships disintegrate — and pray God that will be sooner than any of us now dares to hope — then our country must continue to play its great part in the period of world reconstruction for the good of humanity.

We believe that the rallying cry of the dictators, their boasting about a master-race, will prove to be pure stuff and nonsense. There never has been, there isn't now, and there never will be, any race of people on the earth fit to serve as masters over their fellow men.

The world has no use for any Nation which, because of size or because of military might, asserts the right to goosestep to world power over the bodies of other Nations or other races. We believe that any nationality, no matter how small, has the inherent right to its own nationhood.

We believe that the men and women of such Nations, no matter what size, can, through the processes of peace, serve themselves and serve the world by protecting the common man's security; improve the standards of healthful living; provide markets for manufacture and for agriculture. Through that kind of peaceful service every Nation can increase its happiness, banish the terrors of war, and abandon man's inhumanity to man.

Never, in all our history, have Americans faced a job so well worth while. May it be said of us in the days to come that our children and our children's children rise up and call us blessed.

Joint statement of the President of the United States and the Prime Minister of Great Britain

The Atlantic Charter

(August 14, 1941)

The following statement signed by the President of the United States and the Prime Minister of Great Britain is released for the information of the press:

"The President of the United States and the Prime Minister, Mr. Churchill, representing His Majesty's Government in the United Kingdom, have met at sea.

"They have been accompanied by officials of their two Governments, including high ranking officers of their military, naval, and air services.

"The whole problem of the supply of munitions of war, as provided by the Lend-Lease Act, for the armed forces of the United States and for those countries actively engaged in resisting aggression has been further examined.

"Lord Beaverbrook, the Minster of Supply of the British Government, has joined in these conferences. He is going to proceed to Washington to discuss further details with appropriate officials of the United States Government. These conferences will also cover the supply problems of the Soviet Union.

"The President and the Prime Minister have had several conferences. They have considered the dangers to world civilization arising from the policies of military domination by conquest upon which the Hitlerite Government of Germany and other governments associated therewith have embarked, and have made clear the steps which their countries are respectively taking for their safety in the face of these dangers.

"They have agreed upon the following joint declaration:

"Joint declaration of the President of the United States of America and the Prime Minister, Mr. Churchill representing His Majesty's Government in the United Kingdom being met together deem it right to make known certain common principles in the national policies of their respective countries on which they base their hopes for a better future for the world.

"First, their countries seek no aggrandizement, territorial or other;

"Second, they desire to see no territorial changes that do not accord with the freely expressed wishes of the peoples concerned;

"Third, they respect the right of all peoples to choose the form of government under which they will live; and they wish to see sovereign rights and self-government restored to those who have been forcibly deprived of them;

"Fourth, they will endeavor, with due respect for their existing obligations, to further the enjoyment by all states, great or small, victor or vanquished, of access, on equal terms, to the trade and to the raw materials of the world which are needed for their economic prosperity;

"Fifth, they desire to bring about the fullest collaboration between all nations in the economic field with the object of securing, for all, improved labor standards, economic advancement, and social security;

"Sixth, after the final destruction of the Nazi tyranny, they hope to see established a peace which will afford to all nations the means of dwelling in safety within their own boundaries, and which will afford assurance that all the men in all the lands may live out their lives in freedom from fear and want;

"Seventh, such a peace should enable all men to traverse the high seas and oceans without hindrance;

"Eighth, they believe that all of the nations of the world, for realistic as well as spiritual reasons, must come to the abandonment of the use of force. Since no future peace can be maintained if land, sea, or air armaments continue to be employed by nations which threaten, or may threaten, aggression outside of their frontiers, they believe, pending the establishment of a wider and permanent system of general security, that the disarmament of such nations is essential. They will likewise aid and encourage all other practicable measures which will lighten for peace-loving peoples the crushing burden of armaments.

"Franklin D. Roosevelt."

"Winston S. Churchill."

Address to Congress Requesting a Declaration of War

Day of Infamy

(December 8, 1941)

Mr. Vice President, and Mr. Speaker, and Members of the Senate and House of Representatives:

Yesterday, December 7, 1941 — a date which will live in infamy — the United States of America was suddenly and deliberately attacked by naval and air forces of the Empire of Japan.

The United States was at peace with that Nation and, at the solicitation of Japan, was still in conversation with its Government and its Emperor looking toward the maintenance of peace in the Pacific. Indeed, one hour after Japanese air squadrons had commenced bombing in the American Island of Oahu, the Japanese Ambassador to the United States and his colleague delivered to our Secretary of State a formal reply to a recent American message. And while this reply stated that it seemed useless to continue the existing diplomatic negotiations, it contained no threat or hint of war or of armed attack.

It will be recorded that the distance of Hawaii from Japan makes it obvious that the attack was deliberately planned many days or even weeks ago. During the intervening time the Japanese Government has deliberately sought to deceive the United States by false statements and expressions of hope for continued peace.

The attack yesterday on the Hawaiian Islands has caused severe damage to American naval and military forces. I regret to tell you that very many American lives have been lost. In addition American ships have been reported torpedoed on the high seas between San Francisco and Honolulu.

Yesterday the Japanese Government also launched an attack against Malaya.

Last night Japanese forces attacked Hong Kong.

Last night Japanese forces attacked Guam.

Last night Japanese forces attacked the Philippine Islands.

Last night the Japanese attacked Wake Island. And this morning the Japanese attacked Midway Island.

Japan has, therefore, undertaken a surprise offensive extending throughout the Pacific area. The facts of yesterday and today speak for themselves. The people of the United States have already formed their opinions and well understand the implications to the very life and safety of our Nation.

As Commander in Chief of the Army and Navy I have directed that all measures be taken for our defense.

But always will our whole Nation remember the character of the onslaught against us.

No matter how long it may take us to overcome this premeditated invasion, the American people in their righteous might will win through to absolute victory. I believe that I interpret the will of the Congress and of the people when I assert that we will not only defend ourselves to the uttermost but will make it very certain that this form of treachery shall never again endanger us.

Hostilities exist. There is no blinking at the fact that our people, our territory, and our interests are in grave danger.

With confidence in our armed forces — with the unbounding determination of our people — we will gain the inevitable triumph, so help us God.

I ask that the Congress declare that since the unprovoked and dastardly attack by Japan on Sunday, December 7, 1941, a state of war has existed between the United States and the Japanese Empire.

Message to Congress Requesting War Declarations

Germany and Italy

(December 11, 1941)

To the Congress:

On the morning of December eleventh, the Government of Germany, pursuing its course of world conquest, declared war against the United States.

The long known and the long expected has thus taken place. The forces endeavoring to enslave the entire world now are moving toward this hemisphere.

Never before has there been a greater challenge to life, liberty, and civilization.

Delay invites greater danger. Rapid and united effort by all of the peoples of the world who are determined to remain free will insure a world victory of the forces of justice and of righteousness over the forces of savagery and of barbarism.

Italy also has declared war against the United States.

I therefore request the Congress to recognize a state of war between the United States and Germany, and between the United States and Italy.

Address On The One Hundred And Fiftieth Anniversary Of The Adoption Of The American Bill Of Rights,

"Revival of barbarism".

December 15, 1941

No date in the long history of freedom means more to liberty-loving men in all liberty-loving countries than the 15th day of December 1791. On that day, 150 years ago, a new Nation, through an elected Congress, adopted a declaration of human rights which has influenced the thinking of all mankind from one end of the world to the other.

There is not a single Republic of this hemisphere which has not adopted in its fundamental law the basic principles of freedom of man and freedom of mind enacted in the American Bill of Rights.

There is not a country, large or small, on this continent which has not felt the influence of that document, directly or indirectly.

Indeed, prior to the year 1933, the essential validity of the American Bill of Rights was accepted at least in principle. Even today, with the exception of Germany, Italy, and Japan, the peoples of the world — in all probability four-fifths of them — support its principles, its teachings, and its glorious results.

But, in the year 1933, there came to power in Germany, a political clique which did not accept the declarations of the American bill of human rights as valid; a small clique of ambitious and unscrupulous politicians whose announced and admitted platform was precisely the destruction of the rights that instrument declared. Indeed the entire program and goal of these political and moral tigers was nothing more than the overthrow, throughout the earth, of the great revolution of human liberty of which our American Bill of Rights is the mother charter.

The truths which were self-evident to Thomas Jefferson — which have been self-evident to the six generations of Americans who followed him — were to these men hateful. The rights to life, liberty, and the pursuit of happiness which seemed to Jefferson, and which seem to us, inalienable, were, to Hitler and his fellows, empty words which they proposed to cancel forever.

The propositions they advanced to take the place of Jefferson's inalienable rights were these:

That the individual human being has no rights whatever in himself and by virtue of his humanity;

That the individual human being has no right to a soul of his own, or a mind of his own, or a tongue of his own, or a trade of his own; or even to live where he pleases or to marry the woman he loves;

That his only duty is the duty of obedience, not to his God, and not to his conscience, but to Adolf Hitler; and that his only value is his value, not as a man, but as a unit of the Nazi state.

To Hitler the ideal of the people, as we conceive it — the free, self-governing, and responsible people — is incomprehensible.

The people, to Hitler, are "the masses," and the highest human idealism is, in his own words, that a man should wish to become "a dust particle" of the order "of force" which is to shape the universe.

To Hitler, the government, as we conceive it, is an impossible conception. The government to him is not the servant and the instrument of the people, but their absolute master and the dictator of their every act.

To Hitler, the church, as we conceive it, is a monstrosity to be destroyed by every means at his command. The Nazi church is to be the national church, absolutely and exclusively in the service of but one doctrine, race, and nation.

To Hitler, the freedom of men to think as they please and speak as they please and worship as they please is, of all things imaginable, most hateful and most desperately to be feared.

The issue of our time, the issue of the war in which we are engaged, is the issue forced upon the decent, self-respecting peoples of the earth by the aggressive dogmas of this attempted revival of barbarism, this proposed return to tyranny, this effort to impose again upon the peoples of the world doctrines of absolute obedience, and of dictatorial rule, and of the suppression of truth, and of the oppression of conscience, which the free nations of the earth have long ago rejected.

What we face is nothing more nor less than an attempt to overthrow and to cancel out the great upsurge of human liberty of which the American Bill of Rights is the fundamental document; to force the peoples of the earth, and among them the peoples of this continent, to accept again the absolute authority and despotic rule from which the courage and the resolution and the sacrifices of their ancestors liberated them many, many years ago.

It is an attempt which could succeed only if those who have inherited the gift of liberty had lost the manhood to preserve it. But we Americans know that the determination of this generation of our people to preserve liberty is as fixed and certain as the determination of that earlier generation of Americans to win it.

We will not, under any threat, or in the face of any danger, surrender the guaranties of liberty our forefathers framed for us in our Bill of Rights.

We hold with all the passion of our hearts and minds to those commitments of the human spirit.

We are solemnly determined that no power or combination of powers of this earth shall shake our hold upon them.

We covenant with each other before all the world, that having taken up arms in the defense of liberty, we will not lay them down before liberty is once again secure in the world we live in. For that security we pray; for that security we act—now and evermore.

Fireside Chat 21: A Call for Sacrifice

(28 April, 1942)

My Fellow Americans, it is nearly five months since we were attacked at Pearl Harbor. For the two years prior to that attack this country had been gearing itself up to a high level of production of munitions. And yet our war efforts had done little to dislocate the normal lives of most of us.

Since then we have dispatched strong forces of our Army and Navy, several hundred thousands of them, to bases and battlefronts thousands of miles from home. We have stepped up our war production on a scale that is testing our industrial power, our engineering genius, and our economic structure to the utmost. We have had no illusions about the fact that this is a tough job — and a long one.

American warships are now in combat in the North and South Atlantic, in the Arctic, in the Mediterranean, in the Indian Ocean, and in the North and South Pacific. American troops have taken stations in South America, Greenland, Iceland, the British Isles, the Near East, the Middle East and the Far East, the continent of Australia, and many islands of the Pacific.

American war planes, manned by Americans, are flying in actual combat over all the continents and all the oceans.

On the European front the most important development of the past year has been without question the crushing counteroffensive on the part of the great armies of Russia against the powerful German army. These Russian forces have destroyed and are destroying more armed power of our enemies—troops, planes, tanks, and guns—than all the other United Nations put together.

In the Mediterranean area, matters remain on the surface much as they were. But the situation there is receiving very careful attention. Recently, we've received news of a change in government in what we used to know as the Republic of France—a name dear to the hearts of all lovers of liberty, a name and an institution which we hope will soon be restored to full dignity.

Throughout the Nazi occupation of France, we have hoped for the maintenance of a French government which would strive to regain independence, to reestablish the principles of "Liberty, Equality, and Fraternity," and to restore the historic culture of France. Our policy has been consistent from the very beginning. However, we are now greatly concerned lest those who have recently come to power may seek to force the brave French people into submission to Nazi despotism.

The United Nations will take measures, if necessary, to prevent the use of French territory in any part of the world for military purposes by the Axis powers. The good people of France will readily understand that such action is essential for the United Nations to prevent assistance to the armies or navies or air forces of Germany or Italy or Japan. The overwhelming majority of the French people understand that the fight of the United Nations is fundamentally their fight, that our victory means the restoration of a free and independent France—and the saving of France from the slavery which would be imposed upon her by her external enemies and by her internal traitors.

We know how the French people really feel. We know that a deep-seated determination to obstruct every step in the Axis plan extends from occupied France through Vichy France all the way to the people of their colonies in every ocean and on every continent.

Our planes are helping in the defense of French colonies today, and soon American Flying Fortresses will be fighting for the liberation of the darkened continent of Europe itself.

In all the occupied countries there are men and women, and even little children, who have never stopped fighting, never stopped resisting, never stopped proving to the Nazis that their so-called new order will never be enforced upon free peoples.

In the German and Italian peoples themselves there's a growing conviction that the cause of Nazism and Fascism is hopeless — that their political and military leaders have led them along the bitter road which leads not to world conquest but to final defeat. They cannot fail to contrast the present frantic speeches of these leaders with their arrogant boastings of a year ago, and two years ago.

And on the other side of the world, in the Far East, we have passed through a phase of serious losses.

We have inevitably lost control of a large portion of the Philippine Islands. But this whole nation pays tribute to the Filipino and American officers and men who held out so long on Bataan Peninsula, to those grim and gallant fighters who still hold Corregidor, where the flag flies, and to the forces that are still striking effectively at the enemy on Mindanao and other islands.

The Malayan Peninsula and Singapore are in the hands of the enemy; the Netherlands East Indies are almost entirely occupied, though resistance there continues. Many other islands are in the possession of the Japanese. But there is good reason to believe that their southward advance has been checked. Australia, New Zealand, and much other territory will be bases for offensive action—and we are determined that the territory that has been lost will be regained.

The Japanese are pressing their northward advance against Burma with considerable power, driving toward India and China. They have been opposed with great bravery by small British and Chinese forces aided by American fliers.

The news in Burma tonight is not good. The Japanese may cut the Burma Road; but I want to say to the gallant people of China that no matter what advances the Japanese may make, ways will be found to deliver airplanes and munitions of war to the armies of Generalissimo Chiang Kai-shek.

We remember that the Chinese people were the first to stand up and fight against the aggressors in this war; and in the future a still unconquerable China will play its proper role in maintaining peace and prosperity, not only in eastern Asia but in the whole world.

For every advance that the Japanese have made since they started their frenzied career of conquest, they have had to pay a very heavy toll in warships, in transports, in planes, and in men. They are feeling the effects of those losses.

It is even reported from Japan that somebody has dropped bombs on Tokyo, and on other principal centers of Japanese war industries.

If this be true, it is the first time in history that Japan has suffered such indignities.

Although the treacherous attack on Pearl Harbor was the immediate cause of our entry into the war, that event found the American people spiritually prepared for war on a worldwide scale. We went into this war fighting. We know what we are fighting for. We realize that the war has become what Hitler originally proclaimed it to be—a total war.

Not all of us can have the privilege of fighting our enemies in distant parts of the world.

Not all of us can have the privilege of working in a munitions factory or a shipyard, or on the farms or in oil fields or mines, producing the weapons or the raw materials that are needed by our armed forces.

But there is one front and one battle where everyone in the United States — every man, woman, and child — is in action, and will be privileged to remain in action throughout this war. That front is right here at home, in our daily lives, in our daily tasks. Here at home everyone will have the privilege of making whatever self-denial is necessary, not only to supply our fighting men, but to keep the economic structure of our country fortified and secure during the war and after the war.

This will require, of course, the abandonment not only of luxuries but of many other creature comforts.

Every loyal American is aware of his individual responsibility. Whenever I hear anyone saying, "The American people are complacent — they need to be aroused," I feel like asking him to come to Washington to read the mail that floods into the White House and into all departments of this government. The one question that recurs through all these thousands of letters and messages is, "What more can I do to help my country in winning this war?"

To build the factories, to buy the materials, to pay the labor, to provide the transportation, to equip and feed and house the soldiers and sailors and marines, and to do all the thousands of things necessary in a war — all cost a lot of money, more money than has ever been spent by any nation at anytime in the long history of the world.

We are now spending, solely for war purposes, the sum of about $100 million every day in the week. But, before this year is over, that almost unbelievable rate of expenditure will be doubled.

All of this money has to be spent — and spent quickly — if we are to produce within the time now available the enormous quantities of weapons of war which we need. But the spending of these tremendous sums presents grave danger of disaster to our national economy.

When your government continues to spend these unprecedented sums for munitions month by month and year by year, that money goes into the pocketbooks and bank accounts of the people of the United States. At the same time raw materials and many manufactured goods are necessarily taken away from civilian use; and machinery and factories are being converted to war production.

You do not have to be a professor of mathematics or economics to see that if people with plenty of cash start bidding against each other for scarce goods, the price of those goods goes up.

Yesterday I submitted to the Congress of the United States a seven-point program, a program of general principles which taken together could be called the national economic policy for attaining the great objective of keeping the cost of living down.

I repeat them now to you in substance:

First, we must, through heavier taxes, keep personal and corporate profits at a low reasonable rate.

Second, we must fix ceilings on prices and rents.

Third, we must stabilize wages.

Fourth, we must stabilize farm prices.

Fifth, we must put more billions into war bonds.

Sixth, we must ration all essential commodities which are scarce.

And seventh, we must discourage installment buying, and encourage paying off debts and mortgages.

I do not think it is necessary to repeat what I said yesterday to the Congress in discussing these general principles.

The important thing to remember is that each one of these points is dependent on the others if the whole program is to work.

Some people are already taking the position that every one of the seven points is correct except the one point which steps on their own individual toes. A few seem very willing to approve self-denial—on the part of their neighbors. The only effective course of action is a simultaneous attack on all of the factors which increase the cost of living, in one comprehensive, all-embracing program covering prices and profits and wages and taxes and debts.

The blunt fact is that every single person in the United States is going to be affected by this program. Some of you will be affected more directly by one or two of these restrictive measures, but all of you will be affected indirectly by all of them.

Are you a businessman, or do you own stock in a business corporation? Well, your profits are going to be cut down to a reasonably low level by taxation. Your income will be subject to higher taxes. Indeed in these days, when every available dollar should go to the war effort, I do not think that any American citizen should have a net income in excess of $25,000 per year after payment of taxes.

Are you a retailer or a wholesaler or a manufacturer or a farmer or a landlord? Ceilings are being placed on the prices at which you can sell your goods or rent your property.

Do you work for wages? You will have to forgo higher wages for your particular job for the duration of the war.

All of us are used to spending money for things that we want, things, however, which are not absolutely essential. We will all have to forgo that kind of spending. Because we must put every dime and every dollar we can possibly spare out of our earnings into war bonds and stamps. Because the demands of the war effort require the rationing of goods of which there is not enough to go around. Because the stopping of purchases of nonessentials will release thousands of workers who are needed in the war effort.

As I told the Congress yesterday, "sacrifice" is not exactly the proper word with which to describe this program of self-denial. When, at the end of this great struggle, we shall have saved our free way of life, we shall have made no "sacrifice."

The price for civilization must be paid in hard work and sorrow and blood. The price is not too high. If you doubt it, ask those millions who live today under the tyranny of Hitlerism.

Ask the workers of France and Norway and the Netherlands, whipped to labor by the lash, whether the stabilization of wages is too great a "sacrifice."

Ask the farmers of Poland and Denmark and Czechoslovakia and France, looted of their livestock, starving while their own crops are stolen from their land, ask them whether parity prices are too great a sacrifice."

Ask the businessmen of Europe, whose enterprises have been stolen from their owners, whether the limitation of profits and personal incomes is too great a "sacrifice."

Ask the women and children whom Hitler is starving whether the rationing of tires and gasoline and sugar is too great a "sacrifice."

We do not have to ask them. They have already given us their agonized answers.

This great war effort must be carried through to its victorious conclusion by the indomitable will and determination of the people as one great whole.

It must not be impeded by the faint of heart.

It must not be impeded by those who put their own selfish interests above the interests of the nation.

It must not be impeded by those who pervert honest criticism into falsification of fact.

It must not be impeded by self-styled experts either in economics or military problems who know neither true figures nor geography itself.

It must not be impeded by a few bogus patriots who use the sacred freedom of the press to echo the sentiments of the propagandists in Tokyo and Berlin.

And, above all, it shall not be imperiled by the handful of noisy traitors—betrayers of America, betrayers of Christianity itself—would-be dictators who in their hearts and souls have yielded to Hitlerism and would have this republic do likewise.

I shall use all of the executive power that I have to carry out the policy laid down. If it becomes necessary to ask for any additional legislation in order to attain our objective of preventing a spiral in the cost of living, I shall do so.

I know the American farmer, the American workman, and the American businessman. I know that they will gladly embrace this economy and equality of sacrifice—satisfied that it is necessary for the most vital and compelling motive in all their lives—winning through to victory.

Never in the memory of man has there been a war in which the courage, the endurance, and the loyalty of civilians played so vital a part.

Many thousands of civilians all over the world have been and are being killed or maimed by enemy action. Indeed, it is the fortitude of the common people of Britain under fire which enabled that island to stand and prevented Hitler from winning the war in 1940. The ruins of London and Coventry and other cities are today the proudest monuments to British heroism.

Our own American civilian population is now relatively safe from such disasters. And, to an ever increasing extent, our soldiers, sailors, and marines are fighting with great bravery and great skills on far distant fronts to make sure that we shall remain safe.

I should like to tell you one or two stories about the men we have in our armed forces:

There is, for example, Dr. Corydon M. Wassell. He was a missionary, well known for his good works in China. He is a simple, modest, retiring man, nearly sixty years old, but he entered the service of his country and was commissioned a lieutenant commander in the navy.

Dr. Wassell was assigned to duty in Java caring for wounded officers and men of the cruisers Houston and Marblehead which had been in heavy action in the Java seas.

When the Japanese advanced across the island, it was decided to evacuate as many as possible of the wounded to Australia. But about twelve of the men were so badly wounded that they couldn't be moved. Dr. Wassell remained with them, knowing that he would be captured by the enemy. But he decided to make a last desperate attempt to get the men out of Java. He asked each of them if he wished to take the chance, and every one agreed.

He first had to get the twelve men to the seacoast—fifty miles away. To do this, he had to improvise stretchers for the hazardous journey. The men were suffering severely, but Dr. Wassell kept them alive by his skill, inspired them by his own courage.

And as the official report said, Dr. Wassell was "almost like a Christ-like shepherd devoted to his flock."

On the seacoast, he embarked the men on a little Dutch ship. They were bombed, they were machine-gunned by waves of Japanese planes. Dr. Wassell took virtual command of the ship, and by great skill avoided destruction, hiding in little bays and little inlets.

A few days later, Dr. Wassell and his small flock of wounded men reached Australia safely.

And today Dr. Wassell wears the Navy Cross.

Another story concerns a ship, a ship rather than an individual man. You may remember the tragic sinking of the submarine, the United States Ship *Squalus*, off the New England coast in the summer of 1939. Some of the crew were lost, but others were saved by the speed and the efficiency of the surface rescue crews. The *Squalus* itself was tediously raised from the bottom of the sea.

She was repaired, put back into commission, and eventually she sailed again under a new name, the United States Ship Sailfish. Today, she is a potent and effective unit of our submarine fleet in the Southwest Pacific.

The Sailfish has covered many thousands of miles in operations in those far waters.

She has sunk a Japanese destroyer.

She has torpedoed a Japanese cruiser.

She has made torpedo hits—two of them—on a Japanese aircraft carrier.

Three of the enlisted men of our Navy who went down with the *Squalus* in 1939 and were rescued are today serving on the same ship, the United States Ship Sailfish, in this war.

It seems to me that it is heartening to know that the Squalus, once given up as lost, rose from the depths to fight for our country in time of peril.

One more story that I heard only this morning.

This is a story of one of our Army Flying Fortresses operating in the western Pacific. The pilot of this plane is a modest young man, proud of his crew for one of the toughest fights a bomber has yet experienced.

The bomber departed from its base, as part of a flight of five bombers, to attack Japanese transports that were landing troops against us in the Philippines. When they had gone about halfway to their destination, one of the motors of this bomber went out of commission. The young pilot lost contact with the other bombers. The crew, however, got the motor working, got it going again and the plane proceeded on its mission alone.

By the time it arrived at its target the other four Flying Fortresses had already passed over, had dropped their bombs, and had stirred up the hornets' nest of Japanese "Zero" planes.

Eighteen of these Zero fighters attacked our one Flying Fortress. Despite this mass attack, our plane proceeded on its mission, and dropped all of its bombs on six Japanese transports which were lined up along the docks.

As it turned back on its homeward journey a running fight between the bomber and the eighteen Japanese pursuit planes continued for seventy-five miles. Four pursuit planes of the Japs attacked simultaneously at each side. Four were shot down with the side guns. During this fight, the bomber's radio operator was killed, the engineer's right hand was shot off, and one gunner was crippled, leaving only one man available to operate both side guns. Although wounded in one hand, this gunner alternately manned both side guns, bringing down three more Japanese Zero planes. While this was going on, one engine on the American bomber was shot out, one gas tank was hit, the radio was shot off, and the oxygen system was entirely destroyed. Out of eleven control cables all but four were shot away. The rear landing wheel was blown off entirely, and the two front wheels were both shot flat.

The fight continued until the remaining Japanese pursuit ships exhausted their ammunition and turned back. With two engines gone and the plane practically out of control, the American bomber returned to its base after dark and made an emergency landing. The mission had been accomplished.

The name of that pilot is Captain Hewitt T. Wheless, of the United States Army. He comes from a place called Menard, Texas—with a population of 2,375. He has been awarded the Distinguished Service Cross. And I hope that he is listening.

These stories I have told you are not exceptional. They are typical examples of individual heroism and skill.

As we here at home contemplate our own duties, our own responsibilities, let us think and think hard of the example which is being set for us by our fighting men.

Our soldiers and sailors are members of well-disciplined units. But they're still and forever individuals—free individuals.

They are farmers and workers, businessmen, professional men, artists, clerks. They are the United States of America.

That is why they fight.

We too are the United States of America. That is why we must work and sacrifice. It is for them. It is for us. It is for victory.

Radio Address to the French People on the North African Invasion

Operation Torch

November 7, 1942

My friends, who suffer day and night, under the crushing yoke of the Nazis, I speak to you as one who was with your Army and Navy in France in 1918. I have held all my life the deepest friendship for the French people — for the entire French people. I retain and cherish the friendship of hundreds of French people in France and outside of France. I know your farms, your villages, and your cities. I know your soldiers, professors, and workmen. I know what a precious heritage of the French people are your homes, your culture, and the principles of democracy in France. I salute again and reiterate my faith in Liberty, Equality, and Fraternity. No two Nations exist which are more united by historic and mutually friendly ties than the people of France and the United States.

Americans, with the assistance of the United Nations, are striving for their own safe future as well as the restoration of the ideals, the liberties, and the democracy of all those who have lived under the Tricolor.

We come among you to repulse the cruel invaders who would remove forever your rights of self-government, your rights to religious freedom, and your rights to live your own lives in peace and security.

We come among you solely to defeat and rout your enemies. Have faith in our words. We do not want to cause you any harm.

We assure you that once the menace of Germany and Italy is removed from you, we shall quit your territory at once.

I am appealing to your realism, to your self-interest and national ideals. Do not obstruct, I beg of you, this great purpose.

Help us where you are able, my friends, and we shall see again the glorious day when liberty and peace shall reign again on earth. *Vive la France eternelle*

Casablanca Conference

(Feb 12, 1943)

The decisions reached and the actual plans made at Casablanca were not confined to any one theater of war or to any one continent or ocean or sea. Before this year is out, it will be made known to the world—in actions rather than words—that the Casablanca Conference produced plenty of news; and it will be bad news for the Germans and Italians—and the Japanese.

We have lately concluded a long, hard battle in the Southwest Pacific and we have made notable gains. That battle started in the Solomons and New Guinea last summer. It has demonstrated our superior power in planes and, most importantly, in the fighting qualities of our individual soldiers and sailors.

American armed forces in the Southwest Pacific are receiving powerful aid from Australia and New Zealand and also directly from the British themselves. We do not expect to spend the time it would take to bring Japan to final defeat merely by inching our way forward from island to island across the vast expanse of the Pacific. Great and decisive actions against the Japanese will be taken to drive the invader from the soil of China. Important actions will be taken in the skies over China — and over Japan itself.

The discussions at Casablanca have been continued in Chungking with the Generalissimo by General Arnold and have resulted in definite plans for offensive operations. There are many roads which lead right to Tokyo. We shall neglect none of them.

In an attempt to ward off the inevitable disaster, the Axis propagandist are trying all of their old tricks in order to divide the United Nations. They seek to create the idea that if we win this war, Russia, England, China, and the United States are going to get into a cat-and-dog fight. This is their final effort to turn one nation against another, in the vain hope that they may settle with one or two at a time — that any of us may be so gullible and so forgetful as to be duped into making "deals" at the expense of our Allies. To these panicky attempts to escape the consequences of their crimes we say — all the United Nations say — that the only terms on which we shall deal with an Axis government or any Axis factions are the terms proclaimed at Casablanca: "Unconditional Surrender." In our uncompromising policy we mean no harm to the common people of the Axis nations. But we do mean to impose punishment and retribution in full upon their guilty, barbaric leaders...

In the years of the American and French revolutions the fundamental principle guiding our democracies was established. The cornerstone of our whole democratic edifice was the principle that from the people and the people alone flows the authority of government.

It is one of our war aims, as expressed in the Atlantic Charter, that the conquered populations of today be again the masters of their destiny. There must be no doubt anywhere that it is the unalterable purpose of the United Nations to restore to conquered peoples their sacred rights.

The Teheran Declaration

(December 1, 1943)

Declaration of the Three Powers:

We, The President of the United States, the Prime Minister of Great Britain, and the Premier of the Soviet Union, have met these four days past, in this, the Capital of our ally, Iran, and have shaped and confirmed our common policy.

We express our determination that our Nations shall work together in war and in the peace that will follow.

As to war — our military staffs have joined in our round-table discussions, and we have concerted our plans for the destruction of the German forces. We have reached complete agreement as to the scope and timing of the operations to be undertaken from the east, west, and south.

The common understanding which we have here reached guarantees that victory will be ours.

And as to peace — we are sure that our concord will win an enduring peace. We recognize fully the supreme responsibility resting upon us and all the United Nations to make a peace which will command the good will of the overwhelming mass of the peoples of the world and banish the scourge and terror of war for many generations.

With our diplomatic advisers we have surveyed the problems of the future. We shall seek the cooperation and active participation of all Nations, large and small, whose peoples in heart and mind are dedicated, as are our own peoples, to the elimination of tyranny and slavery, oppression and intolerance. We will welcome them, as they may choose to come, into a world family of democratic Nations.

No power on earth can prevent our destroying the German armies by land, their U-boats by sea, and their war plants from the air.

Our attack will be relentless and increasing.

Emerging from these cordial conferences we look with confidence to the day when all peoples of the world may live free lives, untouched by tyranny, and according to their varying desires and their own consciences.

We came here with hope and determination. We leave here, friends in fact, in spirit, and in purpose.

Signed: ROOSEVELT, CHURCHILL, AND STALIN.

Signed at Teheran, December l, 1943.

Acceptance Speech at the Democratic National Convention

"Make another war impossible"

(July 20, 1944)

I have already indicated to you why I accept the nomination that you have offered me—in spite of my desire to retire to the quiet of private life.

You in this Convention are aware of what I have sought to gain for the Nation, and you have asked me to continue.

It seems wholly likely that within the next four years our armed forces, and those of our allies, will have gained a complete victory over Germany and Japan, sooner or later, and that the world once more will be at peace—under a system, we hope that will prevent a new world war. In an event, whenever that time comes, new hands will then have full opportunity to realize the ideals which we seek.

In the last three elections the people of the United States have transcended party affiliation. Not only Democrats but also forward-looking Republicans and millions of independent voters have turned to progressive leadership—a leadership which has sought consistently—and with fair success—to advance the lot of the average American citizen who had been so forgotten during the period after the last war. I am confident that they will continue to look to that same kind of liberalism to build our safer economy for the future.

I am sure that you will understand me when I say that my decision, expressed to you formally tonight, is based solely on a sense of obligation to serve if called upon to do so by the people of the United States.

I shall not campaign, in the usual sense, for the office. In these days of tragic sorrow, I do not consider it fitting. And besides, in these days of global warfare, I shall not be able to find the time. I shall, however, feel free to report to the people the facts about matters of concern to them and especially to correct any misrepresentations.

During the past few days I have been coming across the whole width of the continent, to a naval base where I am speaking to you now from the train.

As I was crossing the fertile lands and the wide plains and the Great Divide, I could not fail to think of the new relationship between the people of our farms and cities and villages and the people of the rest of the world overseas—on the islands of the Pacific, in the Far East, and in the other Americas, in Britain and Normandy and Germany and Poland and Russia itself.

For Oklahoma and California, for example, are becoming a part of all these distant spots as greatly as Massachusetts and Virginia were a part of the European picture in 1778. Today, Oklahoma and California are being defended in Normandy and on Saipan; and they must be defended there—for what happens in Normandy and Saipan vitally affects the security and well-being of every human being in Oklahoma and California.

Mankind changes the scope and the breadth of its thought and vision slowly indeed. In the days of the Roman Empire eyes were focused on Europe and the Mediterranean area. The civilization in the Far East was barely known. The American continents were unheard of.

And even after the people of Europe began to spill over to other continents, the people of North America in Colonial days knew only their Atlantic seaboard and a tiny portion of the other Americas, and they turned mostly for trade and international relationship to Europe. Africa, at that time, was considered only as the provider of human chattels. Asia was essentially unknown to our ancestors.

During the nineteenth century, during that era of development and expansion on this continent, we felt a natural isolation — geographic, economic, and political — an isolation from the vast world which lay overseas.

Not until this generation — roughly this century — have people here and elsewhere been compelled more and more to widen the orbit of their vision to include every part of the world. Yes, it has been a wrench perhaps — but a very necessary one.

It is good that we are all getting that broader vision. For we shall need it after the war. The isolationists and the ostriches who plagued our thinking before Pearl Harbor are becoming slowly extinct. The American people now know that all Nations of the world — large and small — will have to play their appropriate part in keeping the peace by force, and in deciding peacefully the disputes which might lead to war.

We all know how truly the world has become one — that if Germany and Japan, for example, were to come through this war with their philosophies established and their armies intact, our own grandchildren would again have to be fighting in their day for their liberties and their lives.

Some day soon we shall all be able to fly to any other part of the world within twenty-four hours. Oceans will no longer figure as greatly in our physical defense as they have in the past. For our own safety and for our own economic good, therefore—if for no other reason—we must take a leading part in the maintenance of peace and in the increase of trade among all the Nations of the world.

And that is why your Government for many, many months has been laying plans, and studying the problems of the near future—preparing itself to act so that the people of the United States may not suffer hardships after the war, may continue constantly to improve their standards, and may join with other Nations in doing the same. There are even now working toward that end, the best staff in all our history—men and women of all parties and from every part of the Nation. I realize that planning is a word which in some places brings forth sneers. But, for example, before our entry into the war it was planning, which made possible the magnificent organization and equipment of the Army and Navy of the United States which are fighting for us and for our civilization today.

Improvement through planning is the order of the day. Even military affairs, things do not stand still. An army or a navy trained and equipped and fighting according to a 1932 model would not have been a safe reliance in 1944. And if we are to progress in our civilization, improvement is necessary in other fields—in the physical things that are a part of our daily lives, and also in the concepts of social justice at home and abroad.

I am now at this naval base in the performance of my duties under the Constitution. The war waits for no elections. Decisions must be made—plans must be laid—strategy must be carried out. They do not concern merely a party or a group. They will affect the daily lives of Americans for generations to come.

What is the job before us in 1944? First, to win the war—to win the war fast, to win it overpoweringly. Second, to form worldwide international organizations, and to arrange to use the armed forces of the sovereign Nations of the world to make another war impossible within the foreseeable future. And third, to build an economy for our returning veterans and for all Americans—which will provide employment and provide decent standards of living.

The people of the United States will decide this fall whether they wish to turn over this 1944 job—this worldwide job—to inexperienced or immature hands, to those who opposed lend-lease and international cooperation against the forces of aggression and tyranny, until they could read the polls of popular sentiment; or whether they wish to leave it to those who saw the danger from abroad, who met it head-on, and who now have seized the offensive and carried the war to its present stages of success—to those who, by international conferences and united actions have begun to build that kind of common understanding and cooperative experience which will be so necessary in the world to come.

They will also decide, these people of ours, whether they will entrust the task of postwar reconversion to those who offered the veterans of the last war breadlines and apple-selling and who finally led the American people down to the abyss of 1932; or whether they will leave it to those who rescued American business, agriculture, industry, finance, and labor in 1933, and who have already planned and put through much legislation to help our veterans resume their normal occupations in a well-ordered reconversion process.

They will not decide these questions by reading glowing words or platform pledges—the mouthings of those who are willing to promise anything and everything—contradictions, inconsistencies, impossibilities—anything which might snare a few votes here and a few votes there.

They will decide on the record—the record written on the seas, on the land, and in the skies.

They will decide on the record of our domestic accomplishments in recovery and reform since March 4, 1933.

And they will decide on the record of our war production and food production—unparalleled in all history, in spite of the doubts and sneers of those in high places who said it cannot be done.

They will decide on the record of the International Food Conference, of U.N.R.R.A., of the International Labor Conference, of the International Education Conference, of the International Monetary Conference.

And they will decide on the record written in the Atlantic Charter, at Casablanca, at Cairo, at Moscow, and at Teheran.

We have made mistakes. Who has not?

Things will not always be perfect. Are they ever perfect, in human affairs?

But the objective at home and abroad has always been clear before us. Constantly, we have made steady, sure progress toward that objective. The record is plain and unmistakable as to that — a record for everyone to read.

The greatest wartime President in our history, after a wartime election which he called the "most reliable indication of public purpose in this country," set the goal for the United States, a goal in terms as applicable today as they were in 1865 — terms which the human mind cannot improve:

". . . .with firmness in the right, as God gives us to see the right, let us strive on to finish the work we are in; to bind up the Nation's wounds; to care for him who shall have borne the battle, and for his widow, and his orphan — to do all which may achieve and cherish a just and lasting peace among ourselves, and with all Nations."

Joint Statement with Churchill and Stalin

The Yalta Conference

(February 11, 1945)

THE DEFEAT OF GERMANY

We have considered and determined the military plans of the three Allied powers for the final defeat of the common enemy. The military staffs of the three Allied Nations have met in daily meetings throughout the Conference. These meetings have been most satisfactory from every point of view and have resulted in closer coordination of the military effort of the three Allies than ever before. The fullest information has been interchanged. The timing, scope, and coordination of new and even more powerful blows to be launched by our armies and air forces into the heart of Germany from the East, West, North, and South have been fully agreed and planned in detail.

Our combined military plans will be made known only as we execute them, but we believe that the very close working partnership among the three staffs attained at this Conference will result in shortening the war. Meetings of the three staffs will be continued in the future whenever the need arises.

Nazi Germany is doomed. The German people will only make the cost of their defeat heavier to themselves by attempting to continue a hopeless resistance.

THE OCCUPATION AND CONTROL OF GERMANY

We have agreed on common policies and plans for enforcing the unconditional surrender terms which we shall impose together on Nazi Germany after German armed resistance has been finally crushed. These terms will not be made known until the final defeat of Germany has been accomplished. Under the agreed plan, the forces of the three powers will each occupy a separate zone of Germany. Coordinated administration and control has been provided for under the plan through a central control commission consisting of the Supreme Commanders of the three powers with headquarters in Berlin. It has been agreed that France should be invited by the three powers, if she should so desire, to take over a zone of occupation, and to participate as a fourth member of the control commission. The limits of the French zone will be agreed by the four Governments concerned through their representatives on the European Advisory Commission.

It is our inflexible purpose to destroy German militarism and Nazism and to ensure that Germany will never again be able to disturb the peace of the world. We are determined to disarm and disband all German armed forces; break up for all time the German General Staff that has repeatedly contrived the resurgence of German militarism; remove or destroy all German military equipment; eliminate or control all German industry that could be used for military production; bring all war criminals to just and swift punishment and exact reparation in kind for the destruction wrought by the Germans; wipe out the Nazi Party, Nazi laws, organizations and institutions, remove all Nazi and militarist influences from public office and from the cultural and economic life of the German people; and take in harmony such other measures in Germany as may be necessary to the future peace and safety of the world. It is not our purpose to destroy the people of Germany, but only when Nazism and militarism have been extirpated will there be hope for a decent life for Germans, and a place for them in the comity of Nations.

REPARATION BY GERMANY

We have considered the question of the damage caused by Germany to the Allied Nations in this war and recognized it as just that Germany be obliged to make compensation for this damage in kind to the greatest extent possible. A commission for the compensation of damage will be established. The commission will work in Moscow.

UNITED NATIONS CONFERENCE

We are resolved upon the earliest possible establishment with our allies of a general international organization to maintain peace and security. We believe that this is essential, both to prevent aggression and to remove the political, economic, and social causes of war through the close and continuing collaboration of all peace-loving peoples.

The foundations were laid at Dumbarton Oaks. On the important question of voting procedure, however, agreement was not there reached. The present Conference has been able to resolve this difficulty.

We have agreed that a conference of United Nations should be called to meet at San Francisco in the United States on April 25, 1945, to prepare the charter of such an organization, along the lines proposed in the informal conversations at Dumbarton Oaks.

The Government of China and the Provisional Government of France will be immediately consulted and invited to sponsor invitations to the conference jointly with the Governments of the United States, Great Britain, and the Union of Soviet Socialist Republics. As soon as the consultation with China and France has been completed, the text of the proposals on voting procedure will be made public.

DECLARATION ON LIBERATED EUROPE

The Premier of the Union of Soviet Socialist Republics, the Prime Minister of the United Kingdom, and the President of the United States of America have consulted with each other in the common interests of the peoples of their countries and those of liberated Europe. They jointly declare their mutual agreement to concert during the temporary period of instability in liberated Europe the policies of their three Governments in assisting the peoples liberated from the domination of Nazi Germany and the peoples of the former Axis satellite states of Europe to solve by democratic means their pressing political and economic problems.

The establishment of order in Europe and the rebuilding of national economic life must be achieved by processes which will enable the liberated peoples to destroy the last vestiges of Nazism and Fascism and to create democratic institutions of their own choice. This is a principle of the Atlantic Charter — the right of all peoples to choose the form of government under which they will live — the restoration of sovereign rights and self-government to those peoples who have been forcibly deprived of them by the aggressor Nations.

To foster the conditions in which the liberated peoples may exercise these rights, the three Governments will jointly assist the people in any European liberated state or former Axis satellite state in Europe where in their judgment conditions require (a) to establish conditions of internal peace; (b) to carry out emergency measures for the relief of distressed peoples; (c) to form interim governmental authorities broadly representative of all democratic elements in the population and pledged to the earliest possible establishment through free elections of governments responsive to the will of the people; and (d) to facilitate where necessary the holding of such elections.

The three Governments will consult the other United Nations and provisional authorities or other Governments in Europe when matters of direct interest to them are under consideration.

When, in the opinion of the three Governments, conditions in any European liberated state or any former Axis satellite state in Europe make such action necessary, they will immediately consult together on the measures necessary to discharge the joint responsibilities set forth in this declaration.

By this declaration we reaffirm our faith in the principles of the Atlantic Charter, our pledge in the declaration by the United Nations, and our determination to build in cooperation with other peace-loving Nations world order under law, dedicated to peace, security, freedom, and general well-being of all mankind.

In issuing this declaration, the three powers express the hope that the Provisional Government of the French Republic may be associated with them in the procedure suggested.

POLAND

A new situation has been created in Poland as a result of her complete liberation by the Red Army. This calls for the establishment of a Polish provisional government which can be more broadly based than was possible before the recent liberation of western Poland. The provisional government which is now functioning in Poland should therefore be reorganized on a broader democratic basis with the inclusion of democratic leaders from Poland itself and from Poles abroad. This new government should then be called the Polish Provisional Government of National Unity.

M. Molotov, Mr. Harriman, and Sir A. Clark Kerr are authorized as a commission to consult in the first instance in Moscow with members of the present provisional government and with other Polish democratic leaders from within Poland and from abroad, with a view to the reorganization of the present government along the above lines. This Polish Provisional Government of National Unity shall be pledged to the holding of free and unfettered elections as soon as possible on the basis of universal suffrage and secret ballot. In these elections all democratic and anti-Nazi parties shall have the right to take part and to put forward candidates.

When a Polish Provisional Government of National Unity has been properly formed in conformity with the above, the Government of the U. SS. R., which now maintains diplomatic relations with the present provisional government of Poland, and the Government of the United Kingdom and the Government of the U.S. A. will establish diplomatic relations with the new Polish Provisional Government of National Unity, and will exchange ambassadors by whose reports the respective Governments will be kept informed about the situation in Poland.

The three heads of government consider that the eastern frontier of Poland should follow the Curzon line with digressions from it in some regions of five to eight kilometers in favor of Poland. They recognized that Poland must receive substantial accessions of territory in the North and West. They feel that the opinion of the new Polish Provisional Government of National Unity should be sought in due course on the extent of these accessions and that the final delimitation of the western frontier of Poland should thereafter await the peace conference.

YUGOSLAVIA

We have agreed to recommend to Marshal Tito and Dr. Subasic that the agreement between them should be put into effect immediately, and that a new government should be formed on the basis of that agreement.

We also recommend that as soon as the new government has been formed it should declare that:

1. The anti-Fascist Assembly of National Liberation (Avnoj) should be extended to include members of the last Yugoslav Parliament (Skupschina) who have not compromised themselves by collaboration with the enemy, thus forming a body to be known as a temporary Parliament; and,

2. Legislative acts passed by the anti-Fascist Assembly of National Liberation will be subject to subsequent ratification by a constituent assembly.

There was also a general review of other Balkan questions.

MEETINGS OF FOREIGN SECRETARIES

Throughout the Conference, besides the daily meetings of the heads of governments and the Foreign Secretaries, separate meetings of the three Foreign Secretaries, and their advisers have also been held daily.

These meetings have proved of the utmost value and the Conference agreed that permanent machinery should be set up for regular consultation between the three Foreign Secretaries. They will, therefore, meet as often as may be necessary, probably about every three or four months. These meetings will be held in rotation in the three capitals, the first meeting being held in London, after the United Nations Conference on World Organization.

UNITY FOR PEACE AS FOR WAR

Our meeting here in the Crimea has reaffirmed our common determination to maintain and strengthen in the peace to come that unity of purpose and of action which has made victory possible and certain for the United Nations in this war. We believe that this is a sacred obligation which our Governments owe to our peoples and to all the peoples of the world.

Only with the continuing and growing cooperation and understanding among our three countries and among all the peace-loving Nations can the highest aspiration of humanity be realized — a secure and lasting peace which will, in the words of the Atlantic Charter, "afford assurance that all the men in all the lands may live out their lives in freedom from fear and want."

Victory in this war and establishment of the proposed international organization will provide the greatest opportunity in all history to create in the years to come the essential conditions of such a peace.

Signed:

WINSTON S. CHURCHILL FRANKLIN D. ROOSEVELT J. STALIN

Address to Congress on Yalta

United Nations

(March 1, 1945)

I hope that you will pardon me for this unusual posture of sitting down during the presentation of what I want to say, but I know that you will realize that it makes it a lot easier for me not to have to carry about ten pounds of steel around on the bottom of my legs; and also because of the fact that I have just completed a fourteen-thousand-mile trip.

First of all, I want to say, it is good to be home.

It has been a long journey. I hope you will also agree that it has been, so far, a fruitful one.

Speaking in all frankness, the question of whether it is entirely fruitful or not lies to a great extent in your hands. For unless you here in the halls of the American Congress — with the support of the American people — concur in the general conclusions reached at Yalta, and give them your active support, the meeting will not have produced lasting results.

That is why I have come before you at the earliest hour I could after my return. I want to make a personal report to you—and, at the same time, to the people of the country. Many months of earnest work are ahead of us all, and I should like to feel that when the last stone is laid on the structure of international peace, it will be an achievement for which all of us in America have worked steadfastly and unselfishly—together.

I am returning from this trip—that took me so far—refreshed and inspired. I was well the entire time. I was not ill for a second, until I arrived back in Washington, and there I heard all of the rumors which had occurred in my absence. I returned from the trip refreshed and inspired. The Roosevelts are not, as you may suspect, averse to travel. We seem to thrive on it!

Far away as I was, I was kept constantly informed of affairs in the United States. The modern miracles of rapid communication have made this world very small. We must always bear in mind that fact, when we speak or think of international relations. I received a steady stream of messages from Washington—I might say from not only the executive branch with all its departments, but also from the legislative branch—and except where radio silence was necessary for security purposes, I could continuously send messages any place in the world. And of course, in a grave emergency, we could have even risked the breaking of the security rule.

I come from the Crimea Conference with a firm belief that we have made a good start on the road to a world of peace.

There were two main purposes in this Crimea Conference. The first was to bring defeat to Germany with the greatest possible speed, and the smallest possible loss of Allied men. That purpose is now being carried out in great force. The German Army, and the German people, are feeling the ever-increasing might of our fighting men and of the Allied armies. Every hour gives us added pride in the heroic advance of our troops in Germany—on German soil—toward a meeting with the gallant Red Army.

The second purpose was to continue to build the foundation for an international accord that would bring order and security after the chaos of the war, that would give some assurance of lasting peace among the Nations of the world.

Toward that goal also, a tremendous stride was made.

At Teheran, a little over a year ago, there were long-range military plans laid by the Chiefs of Staff of the three most powerful Nations. Among the civilian leaders at Teheran, however, at that time, there were only exchanges of views and expressions of opinion. No political arrangements were made — and none was attempted.

At the Crimea Conference, however, the time had come for getting down to specific cases in the political field.

There was on all sides at this Conference an enthusiastic effort to reach an agreement. Since the time of Teheran, a year ago, there had developed among all of us a — what shall I call it? — a greater facility in negotiating with each other, that augurs well for the peace of the world. We know each other better.

I have never for an instant wavered in my belief that an agreement to insure world peace and security can be reached.

There were a number of things that we did that were concrete — that were definite. For instance, the lapse of time between Teheran and Yalta without conferences of civilian representatives of the three major powers has proved to be too long — fourteen months. During that long period, local problems were permitted to become acute in places like Poland and Greece and Italy and Yugoslavia.

Therefore, we decided at Yalta that, even if circumstances made it impossible for the heads of the three Governments to meet more often in the future, we would make sure that there would be more frequent personal contacts for the exchange of views, between the Secretaries of State and the Foreign Ministers of these three powers.

We arranged for periodic meetings at intervals of three or four months. I feel very confident that under this arrangement there will be no recurrences of the incidents which this winter disturbed the friends of world-wide cooperation and collaboration.

When we met at Yalta, in addition to laying our strategic and tactical plans for the complete and final military victory over Germany, there were other problems of vital political consequence.

For instance, first, there were the problems of the occupation and control of Germany—after victory—the complete destruction of her military power, and the assurance that neither the Nazis nor Prussian militarism could again be revived to threaten the peace and the civilization of the world.

Second—again for example—there was the settlement of the few differences that remained among us with respect to the International Security Organization after the Dumbarton Oaks Conference. As you remember, at that time, I said that we had agreed ninety percent. Well, that's a pretty good percentage. I think the other ten percent was ironed out at Yalta.

Third, there were the general political and economic problems common to all of the areas which had been or would be liberated from the Nazi yoke. This is a very special problem. We over here find it difficult to understand the ramifications of many of these problems in foreign lands, but we are trying to.

Fourth, there were the special problems created by a few instances such as Poland and Yugoslavia.

Days were spent in discussing these momentous matters and we argued freely and frankly across the table. But at the end, on every point, unanimous agreement was reached. And more important even than the agreement of words, I may say we achieved a unity of thought and a way of getting along together.

Of course, we know that it was Hitler's hope—and the German war lords'—that we would not agree—that some slight crack might appear in the solid wall of Allied unity, a crack that would give him and his fellow gangsters one last hope of escaping their just doom. That is the objective for which his propaganda machine has been working for many months.

But Hitler has failed.

Never before have the major Allies been more closely united—not only in their war aims but also in their peace aims. And they are determined to continue to be united with each other—and with all peace-loving Nations—so that the ideal of lasting peace will become a reality.

The Soviet, British, and United States Chiefs of Staff held daily meetings with each other. They conferred frequently with Marshal Stalin, and with Prime Minister Churchill and with me, on the problem of coordinating the strategic and tactical efforts of the Allied powers. They completed their plans for the final knock-out blows to Germany.

At the time of the Teheran Conference, the Russian front was removed so far from the American and British fronts that, while certain long-range strategic cooperation was possible, there could be no tactical, day-by-day coordination. They were too far apart. But Russian troops have now crossed Poland. They are fighting on the Eastern soil of Germany herself; British and American troops are now on German soil close to the Rhine River in the West. It is a different situation today from what it was fourteen months ago; a closer tactical liaison has become possible for the first time in Europe—and, in the Crimea Conference, that was something else that was accomplished.

Provision was made for daily exchange of information between the armies under the command of General Eisenhower on the western front, and those armies under the command of the Soviet marshals on that long eastern front, and also with our armies in Italy—without the necessity of going through the Chiefs of Staff in Washington or London as in the past.

You have seen one result of this exchange of information in the recent bombings by American and English aircraft of points which are directly related to the Russian advance on Berlin.

From now on, American and British heavy bombers will be used — in the day-by-day tactics of the war — and we have begun to realize, I think, that there is all the difference in the world between tactics on the one side, and strategy on the other — day-by-day tactics of the war in direct support of the Soviet armies, as well as in the support of our own on the western front.

They are now engaged in bombing and strafing in order to hamper the movement of German reserves and materials to the eastern and western fronts from other parts of Germany or from Italy.

Arrangements have been made for the most effective distribution of all available material and transportation to the places where they can best be used in the combined war effort — American, British, and Russian.

Details of these plans and arrangements are military secrets, of course; but this tying of things in together is going to hasten the day of the final collapse of Germany. The Nazis are learning about some of them already, to their sorrow. And I think all three of us at the Conference felt that they will learn more about them tomorrow and the next day — and the day after that!

There will be no respite for them. We will not desist for one moment until unconditional surrender.

You know, I've always felt that common sense prevails in the long run — quiet, overnight thinking. I think that is true in Germany, just as much as it is here.

The German people, as well as the German soldiers must realize that the sooner they give up and surrender by groups or as individuals, the sooner their present agony will be over. They must realize that only with complete surrender can they begin to reestablish themselves as people whom the world might accept as decent neighbors.

We made it clear again at Yalta, and I now repeat that unconditional surrender does not mean the destruction or enslavement of the German people. The Nazi leaders have deliberately withheld that part of the Yalta declaration from the

German press and radio. They seek to convince the people of Germany that the Yalta declaration does mean slavery and destruction for them — they are working at it day and night for that is how the Nazis hope to save their own skins, and deceive their people into continued and useless resistance.

We did, however, make it clear at the Conference just what unconditional surrender does mean for Germany.

It means the temporary control of Germany by Great Britain, Russia, France, and the United States. Each of these Nations will occupy and control a separate zone of Germany — and the administration of the four zones will be coordinated in Berlin by a Control Council composed of representatives of the four Nations.

Unconditional surrender means something else. It means the end of Nazism. It means the end of the Nazi Party — and of all its barbaric laws and institutions.

It means the termination of all militaristic influence in the public, private, and cultural life of Germany.

It means for the Nazi war criminals a punishment that is speedy and just — and severe.

It means the complete disarmament of Germany; the destruction of its militarism and its military equipment; the end of its production of armament; the dispersal of all its armed forces; the permanent dismemberment of the German General Staff which has so often shattered the peace of the world.

It means that Germany will have to make reparations in kind for the damage which has been done to the innocent victims of its aggression.

By compelling reparations in kind — in plants, in machinery, in rolling stock, and in raw materials — we shall avoid the mistake that we and other Nations made after the last war, the demanding of reparations in the form of money which Germany could never pay.

We do not want the German people to starve, or to become a burden on the rest of the world.

Our objective in handling Germany is simple — it is to secure the peace of the rest of the world now and in the future. Too much experience has shown that that objective is impossible if Germany is allowed to retain any ability to wage aggressive warfare.

These objectives will not hurt the German people. On the contrary, they will protect them from a repetition of the fate which the General Staff and Kaiserism imposed on them before, and which Hitlerism is now imposing upon them again a hundredfold. It will be removing a cancer from the German body politic which for generations has produced only misery and only pain to the whole world.

During my stay in Yalta, I saw the kind of reckless, senseless fury, the terrible destruction that comes out of German militarism. Yalta, on the Black Sea, had no military significance of any kind. It had no defenses.

Before the last war, it had been a resort for people like the Czars and princes and for the aristocracy of Russia — and the hangers-on. However, after the Red Revolution, and until the attack on the Soviet Union by Hitler, the palaces and the villas of Yalta had been used as a rest and recreation center by the Russian people.

The Nazi officers took these former palaces and villas — took them over for their own use. The only reason that the so-called former palace of the Czar was still habitable, when we got there, was that it had been given — or he thought it had been given — to a German general for his own property and his own use. And when Yalta was so destroyed, he kept soldiers there to protect what he thought would become his own, nice villa. It was a useful rest and recreation center for hundreds of thousands of Russian workers, farmers, and their families, up to the time that it was taken again by the Germans. The Nazi officers took these places for their own use, and when the Red Army forced the

Nazis out of the Crimea—almost just a year ago—all of these villas were looted by the Nazis, and then nearly all of them were destroyed by bombs placed on the inside. And even the humblest of the homes of Yalta were not spared.

There was little left of it except blank walls, ruins, destruction and desolation.

Sevastopol—that was a fortified port, about forty or fifty miles away—there again was a scene of utter destruction—a large city with great navy yards and fortifications—I think less than a dozen buildings were left intact in the entire city.

I had read about Warsaw and Lidice and Rotterdam and Coventry—but I saw Sevastopol and Yalta! And I know that there is not room enough on earth for both German militarism and Christian decency.

Of equal importance with the military arrangements at the Crimea Conference were the agreements reached with respect to a general international organization for lasting world peace. The foundations were laid at Dumbarton Oaks. There was one point, however, on which agreement was not reached at Dumbarton Oaks. It involved the procedure of voting in the Security Council. I want to try to make it clear by making it simple. It took me hours and hours to get the thing straight in my own mind—and many conferences.

At the Crimea Conference, the Americans made a proposal on this subject which, after full discussion was, I am glad to say, unanimously adopted by the other two Nations.

It is not yet possible to announce the terms of that agreement publicly, but it will be in a very short time.

When the conclusions reached with respect to voting in the Security Council are made known, I think and I hope that you will find them a fair solution of this complicated and difficult problem. They are founded in justice, and will go far to assure international cooperation in the maintenance of peace.

A conference of all the United Nations of the world will meet in San Francisco on April 25, 1945. There, we all hope, and confidently expect, to execute a definite charter of organization under which the peace of the world will be preserved and the forces of aggression permanently outlawed.

This time we are not making the mistake of waiting until the end of the war to set up the machinery of peace. This time, as we fight together to win the war finally, we work together to keep it from happening again.

I—as you know—have always been a believer in the document called the Constitution of the United States. And I spent a good deal of time in educating two other Nations of the world in regard to the Constitution of the United States. The charter has to be—and should be—approved by the Senate of the United States, under the Constitution. I think the other Nations all know it now. I am aware of that fact, and now all the other Nations are. And we hope that the Senate will approve of what is set forth as the Charter of the United Nations when they all come together in San Francisco next month.

The Senate of the United States, through its appropriate representatives, has been kept continuously advised of the program of this Government in the creation of the International Security Organization.

The Senate and the House of Representatives will both be represented at the San Francisco Conference. The Congressional delegates to the San Francisco Conference will consist of an equal number of Republican and Democratic members. The American Delegation is—in every sense of the word—bipartisan.

World peace is not a party question. I think that Republicans want peace just as much as Democrats. It is not a party question—any more than is military victory—the winning of the war.

When the Republic was threatened, first by the Nazi clutch for world conquest back in 1940 and then by the Japanese treachery in 1941, partisanship and politics were laid aside by nearly every American; and every resource was dedicated to our common safety. The same consecration to the cause of peace will be expected, I think, by every patriotic American, and by every human soul overseas.

The structure of world peace cannot be the work of one man, or one party, or one Nation. It cannot be just an American peace, or a British peace, or a Russian, a French, or a Chinese peace. It cannot be a peace of large Nations — or of small Nations. It must be a peace which rests on the cooperative effort of the whole world.

It cannot be a structure of complete perfection at first. But it can be a peace — and it will be a peace — based on the sound and just principles of the Atlantic Charter — on the concept of the dignity of the human being — and on the guarantees of tolerance and freedom of religious worship.

As the Allied armies have marched to military victory, they have liberated people whose liberties had been crushed by the Nazis for four long years, whose economy has been reduced to ruin by Nazi despoilers.

There have been instances of political confusion and unrest in these liberated areas — that is not unexpected — as in Greece or in Poland or in Yugoslavia, and there may be more. Worse than that, there actually began to grow up in some of these places queer ideas of, for instance, "spheres of influence" that were incompatible with the basic principles of international collaboration. If allowed to go on unchecked, these developments might have had tragic results in time.

It is fruitless to try to place the blame for this situation on one particular Nation or on another. It is the kind of development that is almost inevitable unless the major powers of the world continue without interruption to work together and to assume joint responsibility for the solution of problems that may arise to endanger the peace of the world.

We met in the Crimea, determined to settle this matter of liberated areas. Things that might happen that we cannot foresee at this moment might happen suddenly, unexpectedly, next week or next month. And I am happy to confirm to the Congress that we did arrive at a settlement—and, incidentally, a unanimous settlement.

The three most powerful Nations have agreed that the political and economic problems of any area liberated from Nazi conquest, or of any former Axis satellite, are a joint responsibility of all three Governments. They will join together, during the temporary period of instability—after hostilities—to help the people of any liberated area, or of any former satellite state, to solve their own problems through firmly established democratic processes.

They will endeavor to see to it that the people who carry on the interim government between occupation of Germany and true independence, will be as representative as possible of all democratic elements in the population, and that free elections are held as soon as possible thereafter.

Responsibility for political conditions thousands of miles away can no longer be avoided by this great Nation. Certainly, I do not want to live to see another war. As I have said, the world is smaller—smaller every year. The United States now exerts a tremendous influence in the cause of peace throughout all the world. What we people over here are thinking and talking about is in the interest of peace, because it is known all over the world. The slightest remark in either House of the Congress is known all over the world the following day. We will continue to exert that influence, only if we are willing to continue to share in the responsibility for keeping the peace. It will be our own tragic loss, I think, if we were to shirk that responsibility.

The final decisions in these areas are going to be made jointly; and therefore they will often be a result of give-and-take compromise. The United States will not always have its way a hundred percent—nor will Russia nor Great Britain. We shall not always have ideal answers—solutions to complicated international problems, even though we are determined continuously to strive toward that ideal. But I am sure that under the agreements reached at Yalta, there will be a more stable political Europe than ever before.

Of course, once there has been a free expression of the people's will in any country, our immediate responsibility ends — with the exception only of such action as may be agreed on in the International Security Organization that we hope to set up.

The United Nations must also soon begin to help these liberated areas adequately to reconstruct their economy so that they are ready to resume their places in the world. The Nazi war machine has stripped them of raw materials and machine tools and trucks and locomotives. They have left the industry of these places stagnant and much of the agricultural areas are unproductive. The Nazis have left a ruin in their wake.

To start the wheels running again is not a mere matter of relief. It is to the national interest that all of us see to it that these liberated areas are again made self-supporting and productive so that they do not need continuous relief from us. I should say that was an argument based on plain common sense.

One outstanding example of joint action by the three major Allied powers in the liberated areas was the solution reached on Poland. The whole Polish question was a potential source of trouble in postwar Europe — is it has been sometimes before and we came to the Conference determined to find a common ground for its solution. And we did — even though everybody does not agree with us, obviously.

Our objective was to help to create a strong, independent, and prosperous Nation. That is the thing we must always remember, those words, agreed to by Russia, by Britain, and by the United States: the objective of making Poland a strong, independent, and prosperous Nation, with a government ultimately to be selected by the Polish people themselves.

To achieve that objective, it was necessary to provide for the formation of a new government much more representative than had been possible while Poland was enslaved. There were, as you know, two governments—one in London, one in Lublin—practically in Russia. Accordingly, steps were taken at Yalta to reorganize the existing Provisional Government in Poland on a broader democratic basis, so as to include democratic leaders now in Poland and those abroad. This new, reorganized government will be recognized by all of us as the temporary government of Poland. Poland needs a temporary government in the worst way—an ad interim government, I think is another way of putting it.

However, the new Polish Provisional Government of National Unity will be pledged to holding a free election as soon as possible on the basis of universal suffrage and a secret ballot.

Throughout history, Poland has been the corridor through which attacks on Russia have been made. Twice in this generation, Germany has struck at Russia through this corridor. To insure European security and world peace, a strong and independent Poland is necessary to prevent that from happening again.

The decision with respect to the boundaries of Poland was, frankly, a compromise. I did not agree with all of it, by any means, but we did not go as far as Britain wanted, in certain areas; we did not go so far as Russia wanted, in certain areas; and we did not go so far as I wanted, in certain areas. It was a compromise. The decision is one, however, under which the Poles will receive compensation in territory in the North and West in exchange for what they lose by the Curzon Line in the East. The limits of the western border will be permanently fixed in the final Peace Conference. We know, roughly, that it will include, in the new, strong Poland, quite a large slice of what now is called Germany. And it was agreed, also, that the new Poland will have a large and long coast line, and many new harbors. Also, that most of East Prussia will go to Poland. A corner of it will go to Russia. Also, that the anomaly of the Free

State of Danzig will come to an end; I think Danzig would be a lot better if it were Polish.

It is well known that the people east of the Curzon Line — just for example, here is why I compromised — are predominantly white Russian and Ukrainian, they are not Polish; and a very great majority of the people west of the line are predominantly Polish, except in that part of East Prussia and eastern Germany, which will go to the new Poland. As far back as 1919, representatives of the Allies agreed that the Curzon Line represented a fair boundary between the two peoples. And you must remember, also, that there had not been any Polish government before 1919 for a great many generations.

I am convinced that the agreement on Poland, under the circumstances, is the most hopeful agreement possible for a free, independent, and prosperous Polish state.

The Crimea Conference was a meeting of the three major military powers on whose shoulders rested chief responsibility and burden of the war. Although, for this reason, France was not a participant in the Conference, no one should detract from the recognition that was accorded there of her role in the future of Europe and the future of the world.

France has been invited to accept a zone of control in Germany, and to participate as a fourth member of the Allied Control Council of Germany.

She has been invited to join as a sponsor of the International Conference at San Francisco next month.

She will be a permanent member of the International Security Council together with the other four major powers.

And, finally, we have asked that France be associated with us in our joint responsibility over all the liberated areas of Europe.

Agreement was reached on Yugoslavia, as announced in the communique; and we hope that it is in process of fulfillment.

But, not only there but in some other places, we have to remember that there are a great many prima donnas in the world. All of them wish to be heard before anything becomes final, so we may have a little delay while we listen to more prima donnas.

Quite naturally, this Conference concerned itself only with the European war and with the political problems of Europe and not with the Pacific war.

In Malta, however, our combined British and American staffs made their plans to increase the attack against Japan.

The Japanese war lords know that they are not being over looked. They have felt the force of our B-29's, and our carrier planes; they have felt the naval might of the United States, and do not appear very anxious to come out and try it again.

The Japs now know what it means to hear that "The United States Marines have landed." And I think I can add that, having Iwo Jima in mind, "The situation is well in hand."

They also know what is in store for the homeland of Japan now that General MacArthur has completed his magnificent march back to Manila and now that Admiral Nimitz is establishing air bases right in the back yard of Japan itself—in Iwo Jima.

But, lest somebody else start to stop work in the United States, I repeat what I have so often said, in one short sentence, even in my sleep: "We haven't won the wars yet" — with an s on "wars."

It is still a long, tough road to Tokyo. It is longer to go to Tokyo than it is to Berlin, in every sense of the word. The defeat of Germany will not mean the end of the war against Japan. On the contrary, we must be prepared for a long and costly struggle in the Pacific.

But the unconditional surrender of Japan is as essential as the defeat of Germany. I say that advisedly, with the thought in mind that that is especially true if our plans for world peace are to succeed. For Japanese militarism must be wiped out as thoroughly as German militarism.

On the way back from the Crimea, I made arrangements to meet personally King Farouk of Egypt, Halle Selassie, the Emperor of Ethiopia, and King Ibn Saud of Saudi Arabia. Our conversations had to do with matters of common interest. They will be of great mutual advantage because they gave me, and a good many of us, an opportunity of meeting and talking face to face, and of exchanging views in personal conversation instead of formal correspondence.

For instance, on the problem of Arabia, I learned more about that whole problem — the Moslem problem, the Jewish problem — by talking with Ibn Saud for five minutes, than I could have learned in the exchange of two or three dozen letters.

On my voyage, I had the benefit of seeing the Army and Navy and the Air Force at work.

All Americans, I think, would feel as proud of our armed forces as I am, if they could see and hear what I saw and heard.

Against the most efficient professional soldiers and sailors and airmen of all history, our men stood and fought — and won.

This is our chance to see to it that the sons and the grandsons of these gallant fighting men do not have to do it all over again in a few years.

The Conference in the Crimea was a turning point — I hope in our history and therefore in the history of the world. There will soon be presented to the Senate of the United States and to the American people a great decision that will determine the fate of the United States — and of the world — for generations to come.

There can be no middle ground here. We shall have to take the responsibility for world collaboration, or we shall have to bear the responsibility for another world conflict.

I know that the word "planning" is not looked upon with favor in some circles. In domestic affairs, tragic mistakes have been made by reason of lack of planning; and, on the other hand, many great improvements in living. and many benefits to the human race, have been accomplished as a result of adequate, intelligent planning—reclamation of desert areas, developments of whole river valleys, and provision for adequate housing.

The same will be true in relations between Nations. For the second time in the lives of most of us this generation is face to face with the objective of preventing wars. To meet that objective, the Nations of the world will either have a plan or they will not. The groundwork of a plan has now been furnished, and has been submitted to humanity for discussion and decision.

No plan is perfect. Whatever is adopted at San Francisco will doubtless have to be amended time and again over the years, just as our own Constitution has been.

No one can say exactly how long any plan will last. Peace can endure only so long as humanity really insists upon it, and is willing to work for it—and sacrifice for it.

Twenty-five years ago, American fighting men looked to the statesmen of the world to finish the work of peace for which they fought and suffered. We failed them then. We cannot fail them again, and expect the world again to survive.

The Crimea Conference was a successful effort by the three leading Nations to find a common ground for peace. It ought to spell the end of the system of unilateral action, the exclusive alliances, the spheres of influence, the balances of power, and all the other expedients that have been tried for centuries—and have always failed.

We propose to substitute for all these, a universal organization in which all peace-loving Nations will finally have a chance to join.

I am confident that the Congress and the American people will accept the results of this Conference as the beginnings of a permanent structure of peace upon which we can begin to build, under God, that better world in which our children and grandchildren—yours and mine, the children and grandchildren of the whole world—must live, and can live.

And that, my friends, is the principal message I can give you. But I feel it very deeply, as I know that all of you are feeling it today, and are going to feel it in the future.

CPSIA information can be obtained at www.ICGtesting.com

262807BV00005B/82/P